Earth Science!
BEST
SCIENCE
PROJECTS

Environmental Science Fair Projects

Using Water, Feathers, Sunlight, Balloons, and More

Thomas R. Rybolt and
Robert C. Mebane

Enslow Publishers, Inc.
40 Industrial Road   PO Box 38
Box 398   Aldershot
Berkeley Heights, NJ 07922   Hants GU12 6BP
USA   UK
http://www.enslow.com

For Isabel—TR
For Lucy and Marci—RM

Acknowledgment

We thank Jacqui Casey for her help in testing some experiments and Karen Rybolt for her help in developing Experiment 4.1 (Oil Spills).

Library of Congress Cataloging-in-Publication Data

Rybolt, Thomas R.
    Environmental science fair projects using water, feathers, sunlight, balloons, and more / Thomas R. Rybolt and Robert C. Mebane.
        p. cm. — (Earth science! best science projects)
    Includes bibliographical references and index.
    ISBN 0-7660-2364-8 (hardcover)
    1. Environmental sciences—Juvenile literature.
    2. Science projects—Juvenile literature. I. Mebane, Robert C. II. Title. III. Series.
GE115.R93 2005
577'.078—dc22

                                                    2004027016

Printed in the United States of America

10 9 8 7 6 5 4 3 2 1

To Our Readers: We have done our best to make sure all Internet Addresses in this book were active and appropriate when we went to press. However, the author and the publisher have no control over and assume no liability for the material available on those Internet sites or on other Web sites they may link to. Any comments or suggestions can be sent by e-mail to comments@enslow.com or to the address on the back cover.

Illustration Credits: Tom LaBaff

Cover Photo: © 2005 Dynamic Graphics (girl); © 2002–2004 Art Today, Inc. and Hemera Technologies, Inc. (clip art and background).

Contents

Introduction

All creatures, including people, make an impact on the place they live and on all other things that are there—living (plants and animals) and nonliving (air, soil, and water). The place in which a creature lives is called its environment. An environment provides those things necessary to sustain life. It provides air for breathing, water for drinking, and soil for growing food. It provides a surface temperature suitable for life, energy sources, a means to recycle waste, and protection from harmful radiation from space. The earth's environment makes life possible!

The world's rapidly increasing human population and the growing use of Earth's natural resources put enormous stress on our environment. Around the world, people are quickly consuming nonrenewable energy resources such as coal, oil, and natural gas. Nonrenewable resources are those that are used once and are then gone. People are polluting the air through automobile exhaust, polluting the water with pesticide runoff and oil spills, and wasting soil resources by allowing soil to erode. Together we must learn about these and other harmful environmental effects humans can cause. We must learn how to minimize the negative impact on the environment for the present generation and sustain the environment for people of countless generations to come.

HOW TO USE THIS BOOK

The chapters in this book deal with the topics of air, water, soil, pollution, and energy resources. Each chapter has an introduction to the topic, followed by experiments. Each experiment will expand your knowledge of the chapter topic. The experiments do not have to be done in any special order. You can skip around in the book to find the chapters that interest you most. Read the chapter introductions before you perform the experiments.

A section at the beginning of each experiment lists the materials you will need. Most materials are common items in your home or for sale at a grocery store.

At the end of each experiment you will find a section called Science Project Ideas that contains suggestions for additional experiments. You can use the original experiments or suggested further experiments as a great starting point to develop your own science fair project.

You should always use a science notebook when you are doing experiments. Any notebook with bound pages—such as a spiral notebook—will do. Record the date, a description of what you are doing, and all your data and observations. If you are working on a science fair project, your notebook will be an important source of information to show your teacher and judges the work you have done.

Abbreviations and Symbols Used in This Book			
Measurements		**Elements**	
°C	degrees Celsius	Al	aluminum
°F	degrees Fahrenheit	Ar	argon
BTU	British thermal units	B	boron
cal	small calorie	C	carbon
Cal	dietary calorie, or kilocalorie	Cl	chlorine
cm	centimeter	H	hydrogen
ft	feet	N	nitrogen
g	gram	Na	sodium
gal	gallon	O	oxygen
in	inch	P	phosphorus
J	joule	S	sulfur
kg	kilogram		
kJ	kilojoule		
L	liter		
m	meter		
min	minute		
mL	milliliter		
mm	millimeter		
oz	ounce		
qt	quart		
s	second		
W	watt		

SAFETY FIRST

1. Make sure an adult in your household knows what you are doing and has approved your activities. Some experiments are also marked to have an adult help you do the activity. Please do so.

2. These experiments can be done in the kitchen, at home, or at school as part of a science class or lab. Ask a parent, teacher, or other knowledgeable adult if you need help with any experiment.

3. Follow any special instructions given in the experiment or given on the label of any product you are using.

4. Maintain a serious attitude while conducting experiments. Fooling around can be dangerous to you and to others.

5. Never look directly at the sun. It can permanently damage your eyes.

6. Wear approved safety goggles when you are working with a flame or doing anything that might cause injury to your eyes.

7. Do not eat or drink while experimenting.

8. Clean up after each experiment is completed.

9. The liquid in some thermometers is mercury. It is dangerous to touch mercury or to breathe mercury vapor, and such thermometers have been banned in many states. When doing these experiments, use only non-mercury thermometers, such as those filled with alcohol. If you have a mercury thermometer in the house, **ask an adult** if it can be taken to a local mercury thermometer exchange location.

Chapter 1

Air—Our Amazing Atmosphere

We live at the bottom of a sea of air called the atmosphere. Unlike the ocean, this sea is not made of water and salts. Earth's atmosphere is made up of a mixture of gases. Dry air is about 78 percent nitrogen (N_2), 21 percent oxygen (O_2), 1 percent argon (Ar), and trace amounts of carbon dioxide (CO_2) and other gases. Humid or wet air may contain up to 4.00 percent water (H_2O). The atmosphere also contains many small particles of dust.

Through the process of photosynthesis, plants use carbon dioxide from the atmosphere and water from the ground to produce oxygen gas. Green plants use photosynthesis to produce molecules that they use for growth and energy. Animals, including humans, use oxygen and release carbon dioxide. Oxygen and carbon dioxide gases in the atmosphere link plants and animals together in an amazing balance of nature.

Like a blanket, water in the atmosphere helps trap heat energy around the earth and keeps the planet from getting too cold. Carbon dioxide also helps trap heat energy. However, the amount of carbon dioxide and some other "greenhouse gases" has been increasing. The increase in carbon dioxide comes from the burning of fossil fuels such as coal, oil, gasoline, and natural gas. When these fuels are burned, carbon dioxide is released into the air.

Scientists think the continuing increase in carbon dioxide could cause the average temperature around the earth to increase by 2 to 6°F (1 to 3.5°C) over the next 50 to 100 years. These changes could cause sea levels to rise, seasonal flooding and droughts to increase, faster extinction of species, spread of tropical diseases, more violent storms, and possible decreases in food production. On the other hand, when solar photovoltaic cells or wind turbines are used for generating electrical energy, carbon dioxide gas is not produced. Relying more on solar and wind energy and less on fossil fuels could reduce the harmful effects of global warming.

The atmosphere is made of several layers. Temperature differences help define these layers (see Figure 1). The troposphere extends from sea level up to about 16 km (10 mi) and contains most of the atmosphere's air, water vapor, and dust. This lower level is where the earth's weather occurs. The stratosphere extends from 16 km to 50 km (10mi to 31 mi) above the surface. The stratosphere has much thinner air,

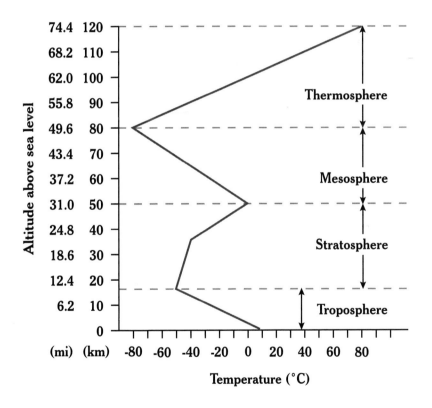

Figure 1.

The four layers of the atmosphere have different temperature trends.

because the molecules are farther apart. Within the stratosphere is a layer with a high concentration of ozone. This ozone blocks a great deal of the ultraviolet light from reaching the earth. This light would be harmful to plants and animals. Above the stratosphere is the mesosphere, which extends up to 80 km (50 mi). Above the mesosphere is the thermosphere, which gradually becomes the same as outer space. The lower part of the thermosphere helps block harmful solar and cosmic radiation from reaching the earth.

Experiment 1.1

Oxygen From Photosynthesis

Materials

- ✓ **an adult**
- ✓ large bucket
- ✓ pondwater
- ✓ permanent marker
- ✓ 3 clear plastic 1-L drink bottles with labels removed
- ✓ concentrated liquid plant fertilizer (10-15-10) with dropper
- ✓ baking soda

- ✓ measuring spoon
- ✓ 3 pieces of rubber tubing 1 m (3.5 ft) long with a diameter of 0.64 cm (¼ in)
- ✓ modeling clay
- ✓ 3 small glass jars
- ✓ 3 small plastic buckets (2.4 L or 2.5 qt size works well)
- ✓ water

The air we breathe is a mixture of gases consisting of mostly nitrogen (78 percent), oxygen (21 percent), argon (1 percent), and a trace of carbon dioxide and some other elements. Plants and animals need oxygen to live. They use it to produce energy.

Oxygen in the air is replenished by photosynthesis, which occurs in green plants. Special cells in green plants absorb light energy from the sun. They use this energy to convert carbon dioxide and water molecules into glucose and oxygen molecules. Glucose is a simple sugar that provides the energy for plants and animals to live. The oxygen is released into the atmosphere.

In this experiment you will try to capture any gas released when algae perform photosynthesis. You will also explore some of the factors necessary for photosynthesis.

You will want to do this experiment when the temperature indoors is close to the temperature outdoors.

In the first part of this experiment, you will grow a thriving population of algae in three labeled bottles. To do this, **ask an adult to help you collect some pondwater in a bucket.** Use a permanent marker to label a clear plastic 1-L bottle LIGHT + BAKING SODA. Label a second bottle DARK + BAKING SODA, and label a third bottle LIGHT + NO BAKING SODA. Fill each bottle with pondwater, leaving about a 4-cm (1.5-in) air space at the top. Add 8 drops of concentrated liquid plant fertilizer to each bottle to supply the algae with the nutrients they need to grow. Cap the bottles and shake to mix. Loosen the caps and place the bottles in a spot outside that gets plenty of sunshine. Check the bottles each day for a week. When the water in the bottles becomes cloudy and green, you are ready to begin the photosynthesis experiment.

Add an additional 5 drops of the concentrated liquid plant fertilizer to each labeled bottle. Add $\frac{1}{4}$ teaspoon of baking soda each to the bottle labeled light + baking soda and to the bottle labeled dark + baking soda. Cap the bottles and shake to dissolve the baking soda in the algae mixture. Remove the caps.

Insert and hold a piece of tubing in the air space just above the liquid level in the bottle labeled light + baking soda. Use modeling clay to completely seal the tubing in the top of the bottle (see Figure 2). To test your seal, place the other end of the tubing in a jar of water and gently squeeze the plastic bottle. If you see air bubbles emerging from the end of the tube in the jar of water, then the bottle is sealed tightly. If you do not see bubbles, check your clay seal and add more clay if necessary. Repeat this process with the other two bottles, making sure to check your clay seals for leaks.

Choose a location outdoors that gets plenty of sunlight to set up part of your experiment. Nearly fill a plastic bucket with water. Submerge a small glass jar into the bucket so that the jar becomes completely full of water. While keeping the jar submerged, turn and hold it so that the open end of the jar is on the

Figure 2.

Insert one end of the tubing into the air space in the neck of the 1-L bottle and seal tightly with modeling clay.

bottom of the bucket. While holding the jar on the bottom of the bucket, carefully pour some water out of the bucket, making sure no air is introduced into the submerged jar. For the experiment, the water level in the bucket should come about halfway up the inverted jar. Carefully insert the free end of the rubber tubing coming from the plastic bottle labeled light + baking soda into the submerged jar (see Figure 3). Make sure no air is introduced into the jar. The tubing should be at least halfway up into the jar. This will allow you to collect any gas that is generated in the plastic bottle. Repeat this process in the same location for the bottle labeled light + no baking soda.

In a dark closet, do the same experimental setup with the bottle labeled dark + baking soda. This part of the experiment will help you determine the role light plays in photosynthesis.

Figure 3.

The setup for collecting any gas generated in the activity is shown above.

Observe your three setups over four days. Do you see evidence of gas forming in all three bottles? Can you actually see bubbles rising to the top in any of the bottles? Do you observe gas formation only during the day? How many days do you see gas forming in any of the bottles?

In these experiments, algae are used to study photosynthesis. Algae are simple, microscopic aquatic plants that play important roles in bodies of water. They are a food source for aquatic animals, and they also supply oxygen through photosynthesis. In fact, most of the oxygen in the atmosphere comes from the photosynthesis of algae in our oceans.

Baking soda, which is sodium bicarbonate, is a source of carbon dioxide. Since these experiments were tightly sealed from the air, which contains some carbon dioxide, the algae in this experiment need another source of carbon dioxide. You should have found that a gas was produced only in the bottles labeled light + baking soda. Unfortunately, you are not able to prove that this gas is oxygen. Using a sophisticated instrument called a mass spectrometer, which is used to identify molecules, the authors proved that the gas generated under the conditions specified in this activity was oxygen.

Did you see any gas generation in the bottle labeled dark + baking soda and the bottle labeled light + no baking soda? What do these results tell you about the role of sunlight and carbon dioxide in photosynthesis?

Does varying the amount or type of fertilizer used in the experiment affect how much oxygen is produced? Try varying the amount of baking soda and observe the results.

Science Project Ideas

◊ Using a 100-mL graduated cylinder, measure the amount of oxygen produced as a function of time. Graph your results, plotting time on the x-axis and volume of oxygen in mL on the y-axis.

◊ Try this experiment with water from different ponds, streams, or lakes. **Make sure to have an adult assist you in collecting the water samples.**

◊ What happens if you place the experimental setup labeled dark + baking soda outside in the sunlight?

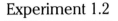

Experiment 1.2

Melting Ice

Materials

✓ ice cubes

✓ 5 sheets of black paper

✓ 5 sheets of white paper

✓ watch

✓ 8 small rocks

Some glaciers are gradually disappearing, and ice around Antarctica is melting. Why is this change happening? Can surface color affect the earth's temperature and ice cover?

This experiment needs to be done outdoors on a warm, sunny day. Place a piece of black paper and a piece of white paper side by side on the ground. Make sure the sun is shining on the papers. Place small rocks on the corners of the papers so that they do not blow away. Wait about one hour and then put identical ice cubes on each piece of paper. Observe the ice cubes as they melt. Which cube melts faster? How long does it take each ice cube to melt? Repeat this experiment at least five times and keep records of how long the pairs of identical ice cubes take to melt each time. Use new pieces of paper each time. Average your results and compare the times.

Did the ice cube on the dark surface melt faster or slower than the one on the light surface?

Infrared radiation (heat) and visible light from the sun warm the earth. You observe light with your eyes. However, infrared radiation is the heat you feel when the sun shines on your skin on a warm day. A darker surface absorbs more of this type of electromagnetic radiation than a lighter surface. A lighter-colored surface reflects more light and heat energy, so it stays cooler.

Polar regions of the earth are covered by white ice and snow. These surfaces reflect a lot of light and heat energy. However, when ice melts, the darker ground underneath is exposed. This dark surface absorbs more light and heat energy and becomes warmer. As the earth becomes warmer due to a less reflective surface, more ice and snow melt. Have you ever been barefoot and stepped from white sand or a cement surface onto a dark asphalt parking lot? What was the difference in temperature between the light and dark surfaces? If you want to stay cooler on a hot day, should you wear white or black clothing?

Albedo means "reflective power." Snow has an albedo of as much as 90 percent (90 percent of light is reflected). In contrast, dark dirt or a dense forest might have an albedo of only a few percent. Oceans absorb light energy, but clouds reflect light. The average albedo of the whole earth is about 30 percent. Much of the light is reflected by clouds before it reaches the surface (see Figure 4).

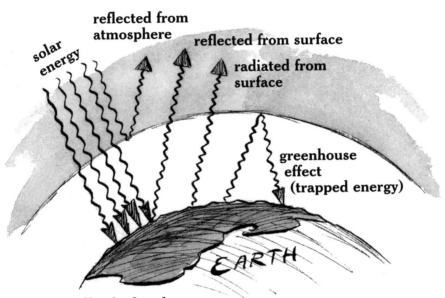

Figure 4.

The balance of solar energy striking and warming the earth and infrared radiation leaving and cooling the earth is complex. If more incoming light is reflected than absorbed, the earth cools. If more incoming light is absorbed than reflected, the earth warms.

- Place identical ice cubes on different surfaces that have been in the sunlight and record how long it takes the ice cubes to melt. Do these experiments on the same day during a time when temperature is constant and there are no clouds blocking the sun. Use surfaces such as dirt, sand, asphalt, concrete, grass, an aluminum pie pan, a white T-shirt, and a dark T-shirt.

- Fill two identical large glass jars—one with dry white sand and the other with dry dark soil. Partially bury an outdoor thermometer in each jar. An outdoor thermometer includes a metal or plastic holder with the scale of degrees marked on it. Record the temperature of each thermometer every ten minutes for two hours. If the temperature reaches 120°F (the top of the thermometer), then stop the experiment. Repeat the experiment on different days. Be sure to record the air temperature each day as well.

    Have an adult help you plot the data you recorded. You can use Microsoft Excel or other suitable software, or you can use graph paper. Plot temperature (°F) along the vertical axis versus time (min) along the horizontal axis. Include a data point for each temperature value recorded. Compare the temperature results for the light and dark materials.

Experiment 1.3

Particles in the Air

Materials

✓ 2 index cards (3 × 5 in)   ✓ 2 plastic bags

✓ clear tape   ✓ magnifying

✓ paper weight   glass

Are there more particles in the air outside a building or inside a building? You can answer this question by collecting and comparing airborne particles from inside and outside a house or apartment.

You will need to make two particle collectors. To make a particle collector, tear a piece of clear tape about 13 cm (5 in) long. Overlap the ends about 1.5 cm (½ in) to make a loop, making sure to loop the tape so that the sticky side is facing out. Press the loop of tape onto an index card just above the middle of the card (see Figure 5). Write OUTSIDE on the particle collector. Make a second particle collector and write INSIDE on it.

Place the particle collector labeled inside on a flat surface in an open room (not a closet) inside your house where it will not be disturbed. Place the particle collector labeled outside on a flat surface in an open area, such as an outdoor table or chair. Place a heavy object on the corner of this card to keep wind from disturbing the collector. If you think it is going to

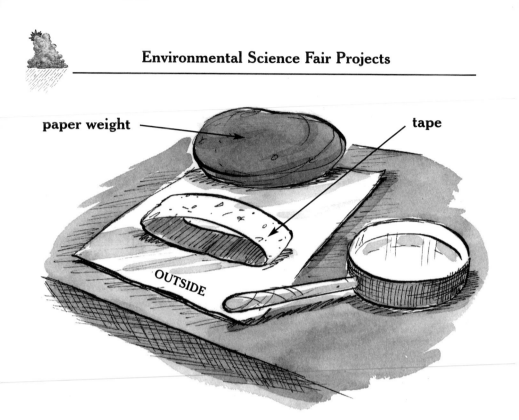

paper weight — tape

OUTSIDE

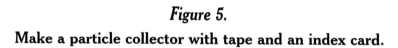

Figure 5.

Make a particle collector with tape and an index card.

rain, move this collector inside and seal it in a bag. At the same time, seal the collector labeled inside in a bag so that both collectors stop collecting particles. Replace both collectors to capture particles when there is no more chance of rain.

Examine the particle collectors each day for a week with and without a magnifying glass. Do you see particles on both collectors? Which collector contains more particles after a week of collection? Do you see different colored particles on the collectors? How would you describe the shapes of the particles on the collectors?

Air is a mixture of gases, but it also contains tiny solid particles. These tiny particles, called particulate matter, consist of dirt, soot, smoke, dust, and liquid droplets.

Particulate matter enters the air by natural processes such as volcanic eruptions, soil erosion by wind, pollen distribution, and forest fires. Human activities also contribute to particulate matter entering the air. Some of these activities include the combustion of fuels in automobiles, trains, buses, trucks and planes; the burning of coal, natural gas, and oil to generate electricity; the plowing of land for crops; the movement of traffic, which stirs particles along the roadside; and the manufacture of building materials. Some sources of indoor particulate matter include cooking, mold growth, breakdown of fabrics, cigarette smoke, pet and human dander, and burning wood in fireplaces.

The particles that make up particulate matter come in a variety of sizes. Fine particles are so small they cannot be seen except with a powerful microscope. Because they are so small, fine particles can stay suspended in the air for long periods of time. Fine particles usually come from the burning of fossil fuels or of biomass such as wood. Coarse particles are much larger and can be seen with a magnifying glass and even the naked eye. Being heavier, coarse particles usually do not stay suspended in air as long as fine particles. Coarse particles are usually added to the air when dust and soil are stirred up by mechanical means, such as cars and trucks traveling on roads or tractors plowing fields.

When you examined your dust collectors, did you see any rodlike particles? Fibers and some soot particles can have rodlike shapes. Soot particles, which usually appear black, may also be granular. Dust and soil particles are also granular. Pollen particles tend to be light colored and usually appear as spheres.

Do some rooms in your home contain more airborne particles than others? Make several particle collectors and place them in different rooms and locations in your house and monitor them each day for a week.

Particulate matter in the air can contribute to air pollution. In fact, particulate matter is one of the six common air pollutants monitored by the U.S. Environmental Protection Agency (EPA). The other five common air pollutants include ozone, carbon monoxide, nitrogen oxides, sulfur dioxide, and lead.

Particulate matter in the air can lead to human health problems. In addition, it can be harmful to plants, other animals, and structures such as buildings and bridges. Scientists are also concerned that particulate matter, particularly soot from trucks and automobile exhaust, can settle on the earth's large snow and ice fields, darkening them. The darker color will absorb more heat from the sun, causing the snow and ice fields to melt more rapidly.

Science Project Ideas

◊ Use these simple collectors to monitor particulate matter for a longer time. Do you see more dust particles on the collectors after two weeks compared to one week? Do you think your results will change depending on the time of year you do the experiment?

◊ Place a particle collector in a drawer or a closet that is not opened often. After one week, compare how much dust is on this collector to a dust collector that was placed out in a room.

◊ Place dust collectors in different outdoor locations. Make sure to label the collector with its location. Some places you could try include a windowsill, porch or deck, garage, picnic table, near a garden, or under a tree.

Experiment 1.4

Removing Dust From Air

Materials

✓ 3 balloons

✓ teaspoon

✓ flour

✓ salt

✓ 3 dinner plates

✓ wool sweater

✓ ruler

Can an electrical charge be used to capture small particles in the air? In this experiment you will use a balloon charged with static electricity to explore this question. Also, you will demonstrate how an electrostatic precipitator removes dust particles from air.

This experiment works best when the humidity is low. Try it on a sunny, cool day if possible. If you do this experiment on a humid day, then the balloon may not become charged when you rub it on a piece of wool.

When you rub an inflated balloon on a piece of wool, electrons—which are negatively charged particles—are transferred from the wool to the balloon. The balloon becomes electrically charged (negative charge). This charge is called static electricity.

Add one teaspoon of flour to a dinner plate and one teaspoon of salt to a second plate. Spread the flour and salt over each plate. Inflate a balloon and tie it off. Hold the balloon over the plate containing the flour. Lower the balloon close to the flour. Do you observe any changes in the flour? Since the balloon does not have an electrical charge, you should see little change in the plate of flour. Now rub the balloon ten times on a wool sweater and place the electrically charged balloon over the plate containing the flour. Slowly lower the balloon toward the flour. What happens to the flour? Does it jump toward the balloon? Does much of the flour stick to the balloon? At what distance does the flour start to jump toward the balloon?

Inflate a second balloon and repeat this activity with the plate of salt. Can a charged balloon attract salt particles? Does much salt become attached to the charged balloon? Does the salt start to jump at the charged balloon at the same distance the flour jumped toward the charged balloon?

Thoroughly mix one teaspoon of flour and one teaspoon of salt on a third plate. Inflate a third balloon and tie it off. Rub the balloon ten times on a wool sweater and slowly lower it over the plate containing the mixture until particles start to jump toward the balloon. Hold the balloon over the mixture until no more particles jump toward the balloon. Turn the balloon over and examine the particles on it. Are there more flour or more salt particles attached to the balloon? Does an electric charge attract flour particles or salt particles better? Why?

Particle pollution is a problem outside and inside homes and buildings. Removing particles from the air in a building is usually done by passing the air to be cleaned over a large filter that is incorporated in the heating and cooling system of the building. Most filters collect only the larger particles, while the smaller particles pass straight through the filter material. Some buildings and homes also use an electrostatic precipitator to remove airborne particles. Electrostatic precipitators use a charged surface to attract dust particles. The particles attach to the charged surface, which is periodically removed and cleaned. Unlike filters, electrostatic precipitators remove even the smallest particles from the air. A properly operating electrostatic precipitator can remove up to 99 percent of the particles suspended in air.

Giant, industrial electrostatic precipitators are often attached to the smokestacks of coal-fired power plants, cement plants, and steel and paper mills to remove soot and other small particles from the combustion gases of these plants before the gases escape the smokestacks. Electrostatic precipitators and other particle-collecting devices can dramatically reduce the amount of particles entering the air from an industrial plant, and therefore lead to cleaner air.

Science Project Ideas

⬥ Collect some flour particles on a charged balloon. How long do the flour particles stick to the balloon? Do flour particles stick longer than salt particles?

⬥ Try this activity with different types and sizes of particles. Try sand, soil, pepper, and sugar.

Experiment 1.5

Greenhouse Effect and Global Warming

Materials

✓ **an adult**

✓ car

✓ outdoor thermometer

✓ piece of string about 40 cm (16 in) long

✓ watch or timer

✓ graph paper

In this experiment, you will investigate what might cause the earth's lower atmosphere and surface to get warm.

This experiment needs to be done on a bright, sunny day.

To begin this experiment, ask an adult to park a car in a place where you can safely open the door. Get an adult's permission before doing this experiment. The car should be parked where there is no shade, where sunlight shines on the whole car.

Place an outdoor thermometer in the shade and wait about five minutes until the temperature is no longer changing. Record this temperature.

An outdoor thermometer includes a metal or plastic holder with the scale of degrees marked on it. This part usually will have a hole in the top. You can thread a 40-cm-long (16-in-long) piece of string through this hole. Tie the string to make a loop. Open the car and put the loop of string over the rearview mirror holder or on some other spot inside the car. Adjust the thermometer so that you can see it when the door is closed (see Figure 6). Make sure all the car doors are closed and all the windows are rolled up. **Stand outside the car where you can see the thermometer, but do not stand in the street when doing this experiment. Stay away from all traffic.**

Start your timer and record the initial temperature (°F) and time at 0 minutes. At one-minute intervals, record the time and temperature. Continue recording these values each minute for 30 minutes or until the temperature has reached the top of the thermometer (120°F). If the temperature reaches 120°F, stop the first part of the experiment.

Figure 6.

What happens to the temperature in a closed automobile on a sunny day?

For the second part of the experiment, roll down all the windows in the car and continue taking temperature readings every minute. Continue for about 20 more minutes.

Plot the data you recorded. You can use Microsoft Excel or other suitable software, or you can use graph paper. Make a plot of temperature (°F) versus time (min) and include a data point for each temperature value recorded (see Figure 7). How fast did the temperature increase? How much did the car temperature increase above the outdoor temperature? Why did the car's temperature increase?

Energy from the sun warms the earth's surface. Most of the energy that reaches the surface is visible light that passes through the atmosphere. However, the energy given off by the warmed planet is infrared (or heat) energy. Infrared energy is a type of electromagnetic radiation that has longer waves than

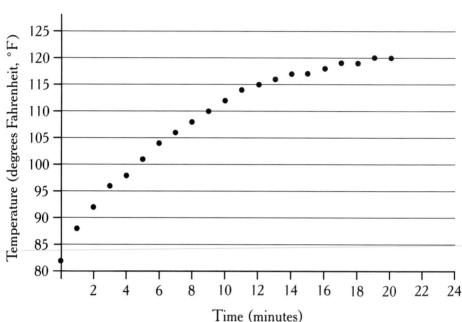

Figure 7.

Plot the temperature of a closed automobile over time.

visible light. This longer wave is blocked by water vapor and carbon dioxide in the atmosphere. If more energy reaches the earth than is radiated back out into space, then the earth will get warmer (see Figure 4 in Experiment 1.2).

Although not identical to global warming, your experiment demonstrates what happens when heat energy is not allowed to leave an object (the car). What happened to the temperature of the car when the windows were closed? What happened when the windows were opened? Every year there are tragic accidental deaths when children or pets are left inside closed cars that get too hot. A child or pet should never be left alone in a closed car.

Scientists have determined that the earth's temperature has increased slightly and will continue to increase because of the buildup of greenhouse gases. Greenhouse gases include carbon dioxide, methane, chlorofluorocarbons, nitrous oxide, and ozone. These gases trap heat, just as greenhouses trap heat in order to grow plants. Over the last two hundred years, the amount of carbon dioxide in the atmosphere has increased due to the burning of coal, oil, and natural gas. This increase in carbon dioxide has contributed to global warming. Can you explain how increasing the amount of carbon dioxide in the atmosphere is like rolling up the windows of a car?

Science Project Ideas

◊ Repeat this experiment on sunny and cloudy days. How do the temperature changes compare?

◊ Repeat this experiment on different days and at different times during the year. How do the results compare in the summer, fall, winter, and spring?

Water—The Liquid of Life

The cells of all living things contain water, and water is essential to keep them living. The human body is about 65 percent water. Humans around the world have a daily need for fresh, clean drinking water.

Although 70 percent of the earth's surface is covered with water, most of this water is salt water. Imagine all the water on the earth being represented by just 100 bottles. Of all these bottles, 97 are filled with salt water that humans cannot drink. Two of the bottles are filled with frozen water, representing the freshwater that is trapped in polar ice, glaciers, and snow. Only one single bottle out of all 100 is drinkable freshwater.

More than half of all freshwater is trapped underground. Freshwater that is trapped underground, above layers of clay or rock, is called groundwater. Groundwater is often found not as free water, but as water filling the pores of rocks and geologic materials. Groundwater is the source of almost half of the freshwater used in the United States. These underground sources of water are called aquifers. Rainwater (and other precipitation) goes down through surface soil and sand to refill these aquifers. The remaining water in all the rivers, lakes, streams, and marshes makes up less than one percent of the earth's total freshwater supply.

Pollution anywhere on the ground tends to enter water because water moves over the surface of the earth and carries pollution with it. Excess fertilizer, pesticides, herbicides, waste chemicals from industrial processes, and even medicines that our bodies do not completely use (such as antibiotics) can eventually reach and pollute water supplies. In many areas around the world, untreated sewage gets into lakes and rivers and contaminates the drinking water. When sewage is treated prior to being released into the environment, and when industries operate with minimum waste, our water sources are cleaner.

Many diseases and illnesses found in developing countries are spread by unclean drinking water. In industrialized countries, water for cities and towns is treated prior to drinking. However, even industrialized countries like the United States sometimes have problems with the purity of their water supplies.

Water on the earth is naturally recycled through the water cycle. Sunlight warms the oceans and surface waters and causes water to evaporate. This atmospheric water condenses into droplets or ice particles and falls as rain or snow, depending on the temperature. When ocean water evaporates, only the water goes into the air, and not the salt, chemicals, bacteria, or other things in the water. Evaporation purifies the water. Freshwater falling on the land replenishes the underground supply as well as the many surface rivers, lakes, streams, and wetlands.

Experiment 2.1

Cycle of Water

Materials

- ✓ **an adult**
- ✓ large frying pan
- ✓ ice cubes
- ✓ measuring cup
- ✓ water
- ✓ red food coloring
- ✓ metal saucepan
- ✓ stove
- ✓ spoon
- ✓ flat pan
- ✓ oven mitt

Have you ever wondered how the water that falls as rain gets into the air? In this experiment you will explore the water cycle and why rainwater is free of the pollutants found in surface water, such as pesticides, herbicides, and animal waste.

Have an adult help you do this experiment. Fill a

large frying pan with ice and wait about ten minutes while the bottom of the pan gets cold. Add four cups of water and four drops of red food coloring to a metal saucepan. Stir until the water is a uniform color. Place this saucepan on a stove and heat until the water is boiling vigorously. Place a flat pan next to the saucepan. **Have an adult use an oven mitt to hold the ice-filled frying pan at an angle above the boiling water. Be careful: The steam rising from the pan is hot and can burn.** The frying pan should be positioned so that water dripping off its cold bottom falls into the flat pan (see Figure 8).

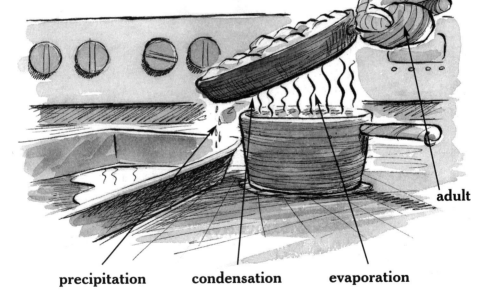

adult

precipitation   condensation   evaporation

Figure 8.

Nature's purifying water cycle can be demonstrated by boiling and collecting water.

Do you see a white cloud of steam above the boiling water? Watch the bottom of the frying pan. Do you see water dripping off the large frying pan into the flat pan? After about five minutes of water collection, turn off the stove. How much water was collected in the flat pan? Compare the color of the original water in the saucepan and of the collected "rainwater" in the flat pan.

The cycle of water in nature is called the hydrologic cycle. The hydrologic cycle includes evaporation, condensation, and precipitation. Heat energy from the sun causes evaporation, in which liquid water in moist soil, lakes, rivers, and oceans changes to gas molecules in the air. You cannot see gaseous water molecules in the air. Rising moist air is cooled higher in the atmosphere, and the water condenses from a gas back to a liquid. Tiny droplets of liquid form around particles of dust. Theses tiny droplets scatter light, causing the white color of clouds. They combine to make larger water drops, or ice particles if it is cold enough. When the water drops or ice particles are large enough, they fall to the ground as precipitation—rain in warm weather and snow or hail in cold weather. Rain, snow, and hail are different types of precipitation.

In your experiment, the white clouds of rising steam were made of tiny liquid droplets of condensing water. In place of solar energy, you used heat energy from the stove to evaporate water. The cold pan condensed the water and allowed drops to fall into the metal pan.

What color was the water you collected? What happened to the red food coloring? Red dye is a molecule safely used to color food. What happens to pollutant molecules found in lakes and rivers when water is evaporated?

Science Project Ideas

◊ Repeat this experiment five times using four cups of water with 4, 8, 12, 16, and 20 drops of the red dye. After each experiment, save samples of the red water in the saucepan and the collected water in the flat pan. Does darker-colored starting water affect the final color of the water after evaporation, condensation, and precipitation? Can you explain your results?

◊ Repeat this experiment with grape soda, orange juice, cola, and apple juice. Collect samples to show the before and after colors. Use your results to help explain why water that evaporates from the ocean falls as pure, non-salty rainwater.

Experiment 2.2

Purifying Water

Materials

- ✓ measuring cup
- ✓ activated carbon (used in fish aquarium filters— can buy at pet stores)
- ✓ clear jar (**do not use lid on jar**)
- ✓ water
- ✓ watch
- ✓ paper towels
- ✓ clear bottle of grape soda

One cup (8 oz) of water contains about 7.6 billion quadrillion (7,600,000,000,000,000,000,000,000) water molecules. If a tiny amount of food coloring is added to water, there could be millions of colorless water molecules for every one colored dye molecule. However, the cup of water would still be colored and not clear because the dye molecules are very effective in blocking specific colors of light. If you wanted to remove these dye molecules to purify the water, how could you do it? You cannot pick them out one by one. In this experiment you will learn how organic molecules can be removed from water. Organic molecules contain carbon atoms and hydrogen atoms, and sometimes other types of atoms as well.

Put one cup of black, activated carbon, which comes in small pieces, in a clean jar. Activated carbon is a special type of carbon that has many small holes and a large surface area. Add two cups of water to the jar. You may see bubbles form as air is released from the porous carbon. Wait about two minutes and gently pour off the water. **Do not allow pieces of carbon to go into your sink drain**. When pouring off the water, hold folded paper towels against the top of the jar. This action allows water to escape while all the small pieces of activated carbon remain in the jar. Repeat this washing process two or three more times. Initially the water you pour off may be blackened from small amounts of carbon dust in the water. Initial darkening of the water is normal. After several washings, the water poured off should be clear and colorless. **Always do this washing to remove any trapped gases on the carbon before doing any experiment with the carbon.**

Pour off as much water from the jar as possible. Next add two cups of purple grape soda to the jar. **Do not put any lid on the jar because some gas may be released and it must be allowed to escape.** Observe the color of the liquid in the jar. Set the jar aside and check the color of the liquid after 3, 6, 9, and 12 hours. Write a description of the color each time you check it. Compare the grape soda in the jar to the grape soda remaining in the bottle. After 12 hours, is the soda in the jar colorless or colored? Can you explain what happened?

Look on the grape soda food label and see the ingredients listed. Grape soda contains two types of dye molecules (food coloring) that are safe for people to drink or eat. These food colorings are Red Dye 40 and Blue Dye 1, which are organic molecules. The mixture of the red and blue makes a purple color that people associate with grape soda.

Activated carbon has many cracks, crevices, and holes. This type of carbon has been reacted with extremely hot steam, which removes many of the carbon atoms and creates a rough and porous solid. The activation process makes many small holes, creating a large surface area where organic molecules can stick (see Figure 9).

Some water companies use activated carbon to help purify or clean water sources being pumped to homes and businesses.

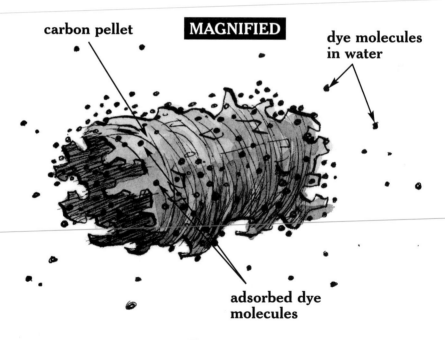

Figure 9.

Dye molecules can be removed from a solution by allowing them to adsorb (stick) on a rough carbon surface.

Some people have filters containing activated carbon to remove organic pollutants that may be present in small amounts in their water supply. Organic pollutants that might be present in lakes and streams include herbicides and pesticides from agricultural runoff, transportation fuels or additives leaking out of storage tanks, oil washed off roads, solvents used in industry, and discarded medicines or drugs.

Once organic pollutant molecules are mixed with water in the environment, they become difficult and expensive to remove. Carbon can help in this removal and clean-up process, but cannot always clean everything out. However, it is much better if polluting chemicals are not released into the environment in the first place.

Science Project Idea

Repeat this experiment using fifteen jars, seven of which contain one cup of washed, activated carbon. Make a series of mixtures, each containing three cups of water and either 1, 3, 6, 9, 12, 15, or 18 drops of red food coloring (red food coloring consists of Red Dye 40 and is sold in grocery stores). Label the jars. Add 2 cups of red water to each jar with carbon, and place one cup of the red water in each of the seven other jars for comparison.

Observe the carbon-containing jars each day for four days. After four days, compare the colors. Label and photograph the before and after jars. Can you determine the maximum amount of red dye that can be removed? Adjust the amounts of food coloring and do additional experiments.

Experiment 2.3

Exploring Acid Rain

Materials

- ✓ **an adult**
- ✓ red cabbage
- ✓ measuring cup
- ✓ distilled water
- ✓ saucepan
- ✓ stove
- ✓ funnel
- ✓ empty 1-L plastic drink bottle with cap
- ✓ 5 small clear drinking glasses
- ✓ sheet of white paper
- ✓ pen
- ✓ measuring spoons
- ✓ clear vinegar
- ✓ 5 clean spoons
- ✓ baking soda
- ✓ unflavored seltzer water (carbonated water)

Did you know that normal rainwater is slightly acidic? In this activity you will learn why normal rain contains acid. You will also use a natural indicator to explore if certain substances are acids or bases.

Tear red cabbage leaves into small pieces, no bigger than a quarter. **Ask an adult to boil four cups of distilled water in a saucepan. Ask the adult to remove the saucepan from the heat and to turn off the stove. Ask the adult to add two cups of the red cabbage pieces to the hot water.** Allow the cabbage and water mixture to cool for one hour. The water should take on a deep purple color. Using a funnel, transfer the purple liquid to a clean, empty 1-L plastic drink bottle. You can cap the bottle and store the purple liquid in a refrigerator for several days.

Red cabbage contains a pigment called anthocyanin that gives the cabbage its red color. Because this pigment is soluble in water (it dissolves in water), you were able to remove it from the red cabbage leaves with the hot water. This pigment changes color when an acid or base is added to it. Substances that change color in reaction to acids and bases are called indicators. In the next part of this experiment, you will observe the color change in the cabbage indicator when an acid or base is added.

Place three small clear drinking glasses on a sheet of white paper (see Figure 10). Next to the glasses write ADDED ACID, ADDED BASE, and CONTROL. Add ⅓ cup of the cabbage indicator to each glass. Add ½ teaspoon of clear vinegar (an acid) to the glass labeled added acid and stir with a clean spoon. What color does the indicator turn? Now add

Figure 10.

Red cabbage juice changes color depending on whether an acid or base is added.

$\frac{1}{2}$ teaspoon of baking soda (a base) to the glass labeled added base. What color does the cabbage indicator turn?

The pigment in red cabbage turns pinkish red in the presence of acids and greenish blue in the presence of bases. The cabbage juice is slightly purple when it is neutral (neither acidic nor basic).

Place a fourth clear glass on the white paper and write next to it CARBONATED WATER. Add to it $\frac{1}{3}$ cup of the cabbage indicator, followed by $\frac{1}{4}$ cup of unflavored seltzer water. Stir with a clean spoon. What color does the indicator change?

Pour one cup of seltzer water in a small saucepan and **ask an adult** to boil the seltzer water for one minute. This will release the gases dissolved in the seltzer. Allow this water to cool for thirty minutes. Place a fifth clear glass on the white paper and write next to it DEGASSED. Add $\frac{1}{3}$ cup of the cabbage indicator and stir in $\frac{1}{4}$ cup of the seltzer water that had been boiled. Does the indicator change color?

Carbon dioxide (CO_2) readily dissolves in water. The gas you see bubbling in a just-opened carbonated drink is carbon dioxide that had been dissolved in water under pressure at the bottling plant. Some of the carbon dioxide that dissolves in water reacts with the water to form carbonic acid (H_2CO_3). It is the carbonic acid that makes the seltzer slightly acidic. You probably observed that the cabbage indicator turned slightly pink when you added acidic seltzer water to it. The seltzer water that was boiled did not change the color of the cabbage indicator because all the carbon dioxide that was dissolved in the water was removed by the heating. Gases are less soluble in hot liquids compared to cold liquids. When you heat liquids that have gases dissolved in them, the gases are released from solution.

The amount of carbon dioxide in the air is between 350 and 400 parts per million (ppm). This means that there are 350 to 400 carbon dioxide molecules in every one million molecules in the air. This does not sound like much carbon dioxide, but it is enough to make normal, unpolluted rainwater slightly acidic.

The strength of acids and bases is measured on the pH scale. Water with a pH of seven (such as distilled water) is neutral: It does not contain excess acid or base. The more acidic the water becomes, the lower the pH. The more basic the water becomes, the higher the pH.

Because of carbon dioxide in the air, normal, unpolluted rainwater has a pH of around 5.7. Acid rain results when other gases mix with water in the atmosphere to form other acidic substances. These other gases are sulfur dioxide (SO_2) and nitrogen oxides (NO_x). Sulfur dioxide mixed with water vapor can lead to the formation of sulfurous acid or sulfuric acid, and nitrogen oxides mixed with water vapor can lead to the formation of nitric acid. Sulfur dioxide and nitrogen oxides are released during the burning of fossil fuels in power plants and in transportation vehicles such as cars, trucks, buses, and planes.

Rain with a pH of 4.3 has been recorded in the United States, and in some countries the pH of rainwater has been found to be as low as 4.2. Rainwater with a pH of 4.2 contains 25 times more acid than rainwater with a pH of 5.7.

Science Project Idea

U se your cabbage indicator to test if other liquids such as lemon juice, orange juice, and apple juice are acidic or basic.

Measuring the pH of water solutions requires a pH meter. Many high schools have pH meters. See whether a school near you has one and ask if you may use it. Once you have access to a pH meter, collect rainwater at different locations and check its pH with the pH meter. Does your rainwater have the same pH as normal rainwater (pH = 5.7) or is it more or less acidic?

Experiment 2.4

Blooming Algae

Materials

✓ **an adult**

✓ bucket, 7.6-L (2-gal) size

✓ pondwater

✓ 5 clean, clear 1-L (1-qt) jars

✓ permanent marker

✓ concentrated liquid plant fertilizer (10-15-10) with dropper

✓ aluminum foil

✓ sharpened pencil

✓ camera

Can nutrients affect the population of algae in pondwater? In this experiment you will explore how a source of nutrients affects the growth of algae.

Have an adult help you collect pondwater in a two-gallon bucket. Label four 1-L jars 0 DROPS, 5 DROPS, 10 DROPS, and 15 DROPS, respectively. Label a fifth 1-L jar 10 DROPS DARK. Fill each jar nearly full with pondwater. Using a dropper, place 5 drops of concentrated liquid fertilizer into the jar labeled 5 drops. Add the correct number of drops of liquid fertilizer to the remaining jars. Fold a piece of aluminum foil over the top of each jar. Punch three holes in the foil on each jar with a sharpened pencil.

Place the jar labeled 10 drops dark in a dark closet. Place the other four jars outside in a sunny spot. Observe the jars every day for two weeks and record your observations in a notebook. Take pictures of the jars to help you document your experiment. After two weeks, pour the contents of the jars on the ground, rinse the jars with water several times, and place the jars in a recycling bin or otherwise properly dispose of them.

What happens to the jars of pondwater that contain the added fertilizer? Do the jars become cloudy? If the jars become cloudy, do some become cloudier than others? Does the water in the jar labeled 0 drops change much with time? What does the jar labeled 10 drops dark tell you about the role of sunlight in algae growth?

Algae are aquatic plants that play an important role in maintaining the health of a body of water. Like green land plants, algae use chlorophyll to convert light energy from the sun into food, in the form of organic material, and oxygen for themselves and other aquatic life in the body of water. The nutrients needed by algae in a healthy body of water are provided by the breakdown of organic material found in the water. This organic material comes from the waste products of living aquatic animals and from dead plants and animals.

Adding excess nutrients to a body of water can overstimulate the growth of algae. An increase in the algae population due to excess nutrients is called eutrophication. When a body of water becomes choked with algae, sunlight is blocked, and submerged aquatic vegetation cannot perform photosynthesis. Less oxygen is released into the water. In addition, some plants and algae die. When they decompose, oxygen that is dissolved in the water is depleted. With too little oxygen dissolved in the water, aquatic life suffers.

The primary nutrient that causes eutrophication is phosphorous. Nitrogen and carbon can also contribute to this process. Runoff from agricultural fields, lawns, golf courses, and sewage treatment plants is a source of excess nutrients.

In this experiment you used plant fertilizer to provide an excess of the nutrients nitrogen and phosphorous to the pondwater algae in the jars. All natural pondwaters contain algae. The algae are what give the pondwater a slight green or brown color. The fertilizer used in this experiment was labeled 10-15-10. These three numbers represent the percentage of nitrogen, phosphorous, and potassium, respectively, in the fertilizer. The larger the number for a nutrient, the more of that nutrient there is in the fertilizer.

Science Project Ideas

⚬ Repeat this experiment but increase the amount of fertilizer added to the jars of pondwater. Is there a limit to the amount of fertilizer that will allow the algae to grow? Why?

⚬ Repeat this experiment using water from a faucet. Do you get similar results as you did with pondwater? Why or why not?

⚬ Repeat this experiment with a fertilizer that contains no phosphorous. Do you get similar results as you did with fertilizer that did contain phosphorous? What happens when you use fertilizer containing different amounts of nitrogen, phosphorous, and potassium?

⚬ Try this experiment with water from different ponds, streams, or lakes. **Make sure to have an adult assist you in collecting the water samples.**

Experiment 2.5

Plants and Salty Water

Materials

✓ **an adult**

✓ 6 small identical flowering plants from a nursery
  (Cooler vinca plants
  work well)

✓ scissors

✓ clean jar

✓ measuring spoon

✓ salt

✓ measuring cup

✓ water

✓ permanent
  marker

✓ 5 plastic cups

✓ camera

✓ index cards

Pure rainwater does not contain salt. In this experiment, you will explore the effect of extremely salty water on land plants. Do you have any predictions of how salt water might affect plant growth?

Obtain six small—less than 30 cm (12 in) tall—flowering plants from a nursery or other store that sells plants. The plants will come in a flat plastic container with six compartments. You need one of these flats of six nearly identical plants.

Have an adult help you cut the plastic flat into six separate containers, with each plant now in its own separate compartment. Notice that each plant container has drain holes in the bottom for excess water. Thoroughly mix two tablespoons of salt with four cups of water. Save this mixture in a jar labeled SALT WATER.

Use a permanent marker to label the five plastic cups A B, C, D, and E. Select the five plants that seem most identical in size and appearance. Keep the plants in their original containers, but place one container and its plant into each cup. The containers will fit only partway down each cup. This arrangement lets excess water drain out of the container into the cup below.

Place the five cups in a sunny window, and water each plant following the directions given below. Write the date on an index card and lean the card on the cups. Take one picture of the five plants together, with the card in the frame. In your science notebook, record the date and time and write a brief description of the appearance, shape, and color of the leaves and flowers of each plant.

Water the five cups with the following liquids: A—nothing; B—2 tablespoons of water; C—1 ½ tablespoons of water and ½ tablespoon of salt water; D—1 tablespoon of water and 1 tablespoon of salt water; E—2 tablespoons of salt water. Each day, water the plants in the same way. Plant A gets no water, while each of the other plants gets 2 tablespoons of pure to salty water. As you go from B to C to D to E, each plant receives more salt in its daily watering. Continue the experiment for at least seven days. Each day after you water the plants, take one picture of the five plants together. Be sure to include a new index card with the date in your photo. Write a brief description of the plants each day in your science notebook.

What have you observed after seven days? Are any leaves drooping, curling, or shrinking? Are there any color changes in the leaves? Have the flowers of any of the plants changed? After the photographs are printed, arrange them in order. What changes do they show? Compare your written descriptions to the photos.

Underground sources of water called aquifers provide about half the freshwater used in the United States. Rainwater and other precipitation filters down through surface soil and sand to refill these aquifers. However, if water is pumped out of an aquifer faster than precipitation can refill it, the water level in the aquifer drops. Salt water from the ocean can move into coastal aquifers and replace the freshwater that was pumped out (see Figure 11). Each liter of ocean water contains about 35 grams of sodium chloride (table salt). Ocean water can quickly contaminate the drinking water.

Irrigation and drainage of desert land is another way that water can become too salty. As surface water evaporates, it leaves behind salt water that is more and more concentrated. From 1930 to 1970, the salt concentration in the San Joaquin River in California increased from 0.28 to 0.45 grams per liter of water. In some places in the United States, the salt level in irrigated fields is so high that the fields can no longer be used to grow crops.

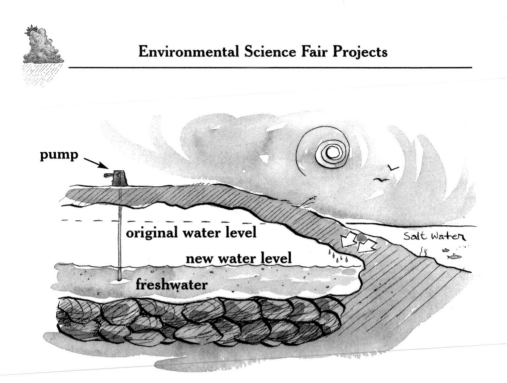

Figure 11.

If too much water is pumped out of an underground aquifer, the water level will fall. If the level of freshwater drops, then salt water from the ocean can enter the aquifer and ruin this source of freshwater.

In the colder parts of the United States, millions of pounds of sodium chloride and calcium chloride salts are used to help melt ice in winter. As snow melts and water flows off roads, these salts get into surface water, including lakes and rivers, and into groundwater aquifers.

Too much salt can affect the growth of plants. In this experiment, high concentrations of salt water were used to produce quicker and more dramatic effects. Did you observe that the more salt used, the greater the effect on the growing plants?

Small amounts of salt are not harmful, but larger amounts can be toxic to plants and animals. The extra salt disrupts the balance of water within the cells of plants and animals.

Science Project Idea

In this activity you will use the salinity of ocean water as a reference. One level tablespoon of salt weighs about 21 grams. One level teaspoon of salt weighs about 7 grams. If you combine three tablespoons and one teaspoon of salt, you will have 70 (21 + 21 + 21 + 7 = 70) grams of salt. Add this salt to an empty 2-L drink bottle and fill with water. You have a salt concentration about the same as ocean water (35 g salt per L of water). (There are smaller amounts of ions from other salts found in seawater that we are ignoring.)

Repeat the original experiment using different amounts of this "ocean water." What is the maximum amount of "ocean water" that can be mixed with freshwater before there is a difference from pure freshwater in plant appearance or growth after three weeks of watering?

Chapter

Soil—Pieces of Earth

In the 1930s, during the Great Depression, the middle part of the United States was called a dust bowl. Swirling clouds of dust often blocked the sky, and clouds of dust settled on the ground. Thousands of people died from illness caused by dust in their lungs. Millions of people migrated to other areas such as California. Because of poor farming practices and dry weather, 9.1 trillion (9,100,000,000,000) kg, or 20 trillion pounds, of topsoil were lost due to wind erosion. Topsoil is the layer of soil with the most organic matter and nutrients.

Soil contains different combinations of three types of inorganic particles—sand, silt, and clay—plus humus. Sand is made of particles from 0.05 to 2 mm across. Silt is made of particles that are 0.002 to 0.05 mm in size. And clay is made of particles smaller than 0.002 mm. To cover a line 25 mm (1 in) long would require 12 or more sand particles, 500 or more silt particles, or more than 12,700 tiny clay particles. Soil also contains air and water within the particle mix.

Humus is a sticky dark organic material made of decomposed plants and animals or animal waste. Humus helps hold the sand, silt, and clay particles together, and it stores moisture and provides essential nutrients to plant roots. The amount of humus varies in different types of soil.

Sand, silt, and clay particles are made over time by erosion of rocks. Sand is often made from granite or rocks containing quartz (silicon dioxide). Clay can be made from rocks containing minerals such as feldspar, which is made of aluminum silicates. Metal atoms can give clay different colors. For example, iron can make clay red.

The movement of air or water, along with chemical reactions, causes larger rocks to slowly break down to the smaller particles of sand, silt, and clay found in soil. However, wind or flowing water can also carry away soil. This type of erosion causes the loss of valuable soil from croplands around the world. Soil is a vital part of the biosphere because it is filled with many different living organisms and because it supports plant growth. Sustainable agricultural practices such as preventing erosion of topsoil and returning nutrients to the ground are extremely important to protect the soil on which all people depend for food.

Experiment 3.1

Layers and Types of Soil

Materials

✓ **an adult**

✓ grassy area

✓ several sheets of newspaper

✓ shovel

✓ ruler

✓ magnifying glass

✓ camera

What is soil? To answer this question, you can dig a hole in a grassy area and then carefully examine the walls of your hole to develop a "soil profile."

Ask an adult to help you choose a grassy area in which to dig a hole. Choose a place that has not been recently disturbed or developed. Also, you may need the adult to help you dig the hole.

Spread sheets of newspapers next to the area where you will dig. Using the shovel, carefully remove clumps of grass in a circle about two feet in diameter. Place the clumps of grass next to the newspapers. Now dig a hole about two feet deep, trying to keep the sides of the hole smooth and straight up and down. Place the soil on the sheets of newspaper.

Starting at the top, use a magnifying glass to carefully examine the soil in the wall of your hole. Do you see any differences in the soil wall as you move to the bottom of your hole? Is the soil darker near the top or bottom of the hole? How many different layers are present in the soil wall? If there are different layers of soil in the wall, how thick (in inches) are the layers? Do you see any living creatures in the different layers of soil? If you see living creatures, in which layer of soil are they mostly found? Use a camera to help you document your observations.

To determine exactly the types of soil in your hole, you would need to have a soil analysis done on the different soil layers. However, you can learn about the composition of different soil layers by rubbing some soil between your fingers and thumb. To do this test, moisten your fingers and thumb with water. Next, take a pinch about the size of a pencil eraser from one of the layers and rub it between your moist fingers and thumb for thirty seconds. If the soil feels spongy as you rub it, then it contains a high level of organic material. If it feels gritty, then it contains mostly sand. If it feels smooth and slippery, then it contains small particles of silt and clay. Do this test for each different layer of soil in your hole, and write down your observations. Wash your hands after handling the soil. When you complete your observations, fill in the hole with the dirt on the newspaper, return any animals, and replace the clumps of grass.

Repeat this activity by studying the soil profile in a wooded area. Do you find more organic material in the topsoil because of decaying leaves?

Repeat this activity in other areas and compare your results.

Soils usually form in distinct layers. A soil profile consists of the identification and composition of these different soil layers. The topmost layer, called topsoil, is usually the darkest layer and ranges in thickness from about an inch to several inches. The topsoil is most important for plant life because it contains much of the necessary nutrients. The dark color of the topsoil comes from organic material in it.

Subsoil is found just below the topsoil. It may consist of several different layers or just one deep layer. Subsoil can reach several feet deep. It is usually lighter in color because it contains much less organic material. Because subsoil contains mostly sand and clay particles and little organic material, it is denser than topsoil.

Below the subsoil is the rocky material that makes the mineral parts of soil. This rocky material gradually breaks down into subsoil and is therefore often called the parent material. Your hole may not be deep enough to see the parent material of your soil. Below the parent material layer is bedrock.

Experiment 3.2

Recipe for Soil

Materials

✓ **an adult**

✓ tall, narrow jar with lid

✓ spade or shovel

✓ soil to sample

✓ water

✓ ruler

✓ sand

✓ clay soil from the ground

✓ phone book

Cake recipes list all the ingredients that go into the cake. Just as there are many types of cakes, there are many different kinds of soil, made with many different ingredients. In fact, there are thousands of different soil types around the world.

In this simple experiment, you can find the recipe for a sample of soil. You will test the soil around your home or school, or in a park, to determine its composition. **Be sure to have permission to dig a hole. Have an adult help you find safe places to dig.** After your observations, return all the soil and any animals you unearth to the hole you dug. Rinse the jar outside and not in a sink.

Dig a hole in the ground at least 30 cm (12 in) deep. You should observe a soil profile (see Experiment 3.1), with darker soil at the top and lighter soil underneath. Remove soil from the bottom of the hole and fill a tall narrow jar about halfway with dirt. Add enough water to nearly fill the jar. Leave a space of an inch (2.5 cm) at the top of the jar. Tighten the lid on the jar, turn the jar upside down, and vigorously shake it for about 20 seconds. Turn the jar sideways and shake it for another 20 seconds.

Set the jar in a safe spot. Return the next day, when the soil will have completely settled into place. Observe the layers. The heaviest layer of soil is sand, the next is silt, and the lightest is clay. If your soil has all these ingredients, then you should see three layers, with sand at the bottom, silt above it, and clay at the top. You may observe fewer layers. Lighter organic material may float on the top of the water; however, humus may soak up water and settle to the bottom with heavy particles.

Sandy soil drains well because there are large spaces between the particles. It does not store water well and dries out quickly. Clay soils can store water well because of the small spaces between the tiny, tightly packed particles. However, clay soils can be difficult to dig into and work with because the particles are packed so close together. Loam is a general type of soil that has a particular combination of sand, silt, and clay (see Figure 12). It works well for farming and crop growth because its combination of larger and smaller particles is loose but still retains moisture.

You can create a simulated soil sample by mixing equal amounts of sand and clay soil in a jar. Add water to the jar and shake. Do the sand and clay settle into two layers, with the larger sand particles beneath the smaller clay particles (see Figure 13)?

Test soil in as many different areas as possible around where you live. Make a chart of how the type of soil varies with the location and use of the land. Draw a picture or make

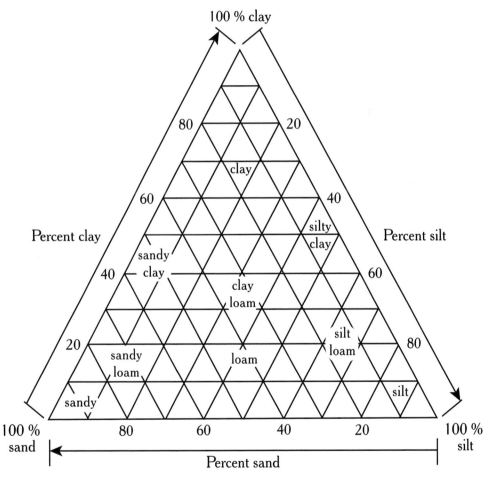

Figure 12.

The inorganic part of soil is a mixture of clay, silt, and sand.

a photograph of each soil test that you can do. Measure the layers to compare the amount of sand, silt, and clay in each sample. Look in your phone book and find the listings for your local county government. If an agricultural extension service is listed, call them and ask if they can give you information about the soil types in your county.

You can add another variable to your investigation. Take soil samples from different depths. Is there a way to compare how the amount of

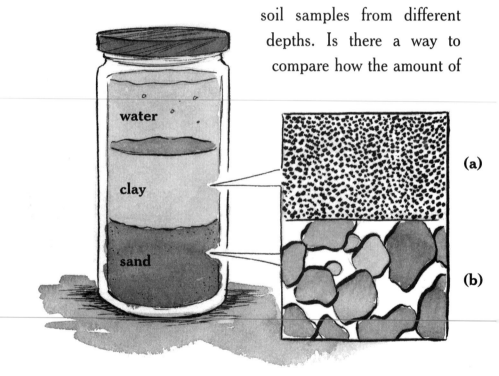

Figure 13.

A soil mixture of clay and sand can be separated into two different layers. Clay (a) is made of much smaller particles than sand (b). The smaller particles have less space in which to trap water or air.

organic material (humus) and the inorganic composition (sand, silt, clay) change as you go from the surface down to depths of 7.6 cm (3 in), 15.2 (6 in), 30.5 (12 in), 45.7 (18 in), and 61 cm (24 in)?

Experiment 3.3

Acidity of Soil

Materials

✓ **an adult**

✓ soil pH meter or test kit

✓ spade or shovel

✓ distilled water if test kit requires

✓ safety glasses

✓ disposable gloves

In this experiment you will test the soil around your home or in a park to determine its acidity. The level of acidity will be measured by a value called pH. The pH scale is usually considered to range from 0 to 14. A pH value below 4 is very acidic, from 4 to 6 is somewhat acidic, from 6 to 7 is slightly acidic, at 7 is neutral, from 7 to 8 is slightly basic (alkaline), from 8 to 10 is somewhat basic, and above 10 is very basic.

You can buy an inexpensive soil pH meter or a soil pH test kit from a store that sells plants and garden supplies. **Follow the directions and any safety warnings on the package. Have an adult help you with this experiment.**

If using a meter, you can insert the probes into the soil, following the directions given on the package, and read the numerical pH value on the meter. If using a pH test kit, first dig a small hole and then place some dirt in the test tube that comes in the kit. Follow the kit directions, and add a liquid chemical or water and a chemical powder to the soil in the test tube. **Do not get any chemicals on your skin or in your eyes. Use safety glasses and disposable gloves.** You should observe a color change. A chart that comes with the kit will show you how to convert the color to the pH value. What is the pH of your soil sample?

Test soil pH in as many different areas as possible around where you live. Make a chart of how pH varies with the location, land use, and type of soil.

Different types of plants grow best in different levels of acidity (see Figure 14). If the pH is either too high or too low, then fertilizer is wasted because nutrients needed by the plant cannot be taken into the plant effectively. Also, disease and insect damage is more likely.

Hydrangeas are colorful and interesting plants that have their own built-in pH meter. When a hydrangea is in soil that has a pH around 4 or 5, its flowers will be blue. However, if the same plant is in soil that has a pH of around 6 or 7, then its flowers will be pink.

Plants in soil that is too basic may lose color and stop growing. The leaves of plants in soil that is too acidic may wilt and

SOIL ACIDITY FOR DIFFERENT PLANTS	
Plant	**Ideal pH Range**
Azalea	4.5–6.0
Bermuda Grass	6.0–7.0
Carrot	5.5–7.0
Centipede Grass	4.5–5.5
Geranium	6.0–8.0
Hydrangea (blue)	4.0–5.0
Hydrangea (pink)	6.0–7.0
Lettuce	6.0–7.0
Onion	6.0–7.0
Pansy	5.5–7.0
Potato	4.5–6.0
Rhododendron	4.5–6.0
Rose	5.5–7.0
Tall Fescue Grass	6.0–7.0
Tomato	5.5–7.5
Zoysia Grass	6.0–7.0

Figure 14.

This table shows the best range of pH for growing certain plants. Hydrangeas can have blue or pink flowers depending on the soil acidity.

fall off. Lime (calcium oxide) can be added to soil to make the soil more basic, increasing its pH. Iron sulfate can be added to make the soil more acidic, lowering its pH. After the chemicals are added to the outside ground, it may take 30 to 60 days before the pH level changes. **Chemicals used to change soil pH should be handled only by an adult who is following the safety rules on the container.**

Experiment 3.4

Erosion—Here Today and Gone Tomorrow

Materials

✓ **an adult**

✓ shovel

✓ patch of growing grass

✓ 2 aluminum pie pans

✓ electric fan with extension cord

When soil is lost from an area due to erosion, it is a serious problem, because all people depend on soil for plant growth and therefore their food supply. In this experiment you will study causes of soil erosion.

Have an adult help you find a safe place to dig, and have him or her help you with this experiment. Dig up a patch of grass, with roots and dirt attached, about the size of an aluminum pie pan. Place this patch of grass-covered ground in a pie pan. Dig up an equal amount of loose, dry soil from the area where the grass patch was removed and fill a second pie pan.

Place the two pie pans side by side on the ground outside. Set a fan about two feet away from the pie pans (see Figure 15). Plug in the fan and turn it on. What happens to the soil in each pan? Try moving the fan closer or farther away. Try higher or lower settings on the fan. What happens to the grass-covered soil and to the bare soil?

Figure 15.

How does the amount of soil loss from wind erosion compare for bare soil and grass-covered soil?

When forests are cleared, trees are removed and their roots die. If the ground is left bare from lack of trees, then water and wind can erode the soil. This can become a serious problem. Sometimes mud slides wash huge amounts of ground off the sides of cleared hills and mountains.

Science Project Idea

R aise one side of both pie pans to equal heights using small rocks as supports. Blow a fan or pour water across both pans. Compare the effects of moving air, flowing water, and the slope of the ground on the amount of erosion that occurs. Try to determine a way to collect and observe the amount of soil eroded under different conditions. Make a table of all your results.

Pollution— Problems of Waste

Nearly everything humans do produces some type of waste. For example, what happens to the candy wrapper, the empty drink bottle, the worn-out piece of clothing, the water when a toilet is flushed, the kitchen scraps, or the dead flashlight battery? If these materials, along with all the other waste materials generated by human activity, are not dealt with properly, they can contribute to pollution.

Waste materials only become a problem when they accumulate faster than the environment can either break down, recycle, or disperse their chemical components. For example, chemical fertilizers are used by farmers to maximize crop yields to help feed many people. If the fertilizer is not applied properly and is allowed to run off the farmland and enter a body of water, it becomes a waste problem. The waste fertilizer could overstimulate the growth of algae in the water, which in turn could harm aquatic life in the body of water (see Experiment 2.4).

There are different types of pollution. Soil pollution refers to dirt that will not support the growth of plants because it is contaminated with chemicals or industrial waste. Radiation from nuclear waste can also be a source of pollution. However, the two major forms of pollution are air and water pollution.

AIR POLLUTION

Air becomes polluted from both natural and human activities. Erupting volcanoes spew large amounts of harmful gases and particles into the atmosphere. These particles can be carried huge distances by winds. Some of these gases include carbon dioxide (a greenhouse gas), sulfur dioxide (a cause of acid rain), and carbon monoxide (a poison). The largest human activity that contributes to air pollution is the burning of fossil fuels such as oil, natural gas, and coal. Fossil fuels provide over 80 percent of the world's energy needs. They are used to make electricity and to provide energy for manufacturing plants. Cars, trucks, buses, planes, and construction equipment also heavily depend on fuels derived from oil. The exhaust from these vehicles contributes to air pollution.

Carbon dioxide is the major waste gas produced when fossil fuels are burned. Although green plants depend on carbon dioxide for photosynthesis, more carbon dioxide is being released into the atmosphere than is removed through photosynthesis. Thus, the amount of carbon dioxide in the atmosphere has gradually increased over the last century, and scientists believe that this increase contributes to global warming.

Sulfur dioxide is another gas that can be produced when fossil fuels burn, particularly certain types of coal. Once in the atmosphere, sulfur dioxide can react with oxygen and water to produce sulfuric acid, which is a major component of acid rain. Today, many industries that burn coal try to remove much of the sulfur dioxide from the combustion gases before these gases are released into the atmosphere.

Nitrogen oxide gases, commonly referred to as NO_x gases, form when fossil fuels are burned at high temperatures, such as in motor vehicle engines. One particular nitrogen oxide, called nitrogen dioxide, NO_2, can appear as a brownish haze that hovers over cities. Nitrogen oxides contribute to acid rain formation and also promote ground-level ozone formation, which can cause respiratory ailments.

WATER POLLUTION

All living organisms depend on water for their survival. When water becomes polluted, quality of life can be jeopardized.

Water quality is a measure of substances dissolved or suspended in water. All natural waters contain substances either dissolved or suspended in them. Some of these substances include gases such as air and carbon dioxide, solids such as sand and clay, certain salts from the soil, organic matter from plants and animals, and microorganisms. Water quality can decline when an excess of any of these substances is added to a body of water.

Major sources of water pollution include seepage from septic tanks and landfills, oil spills, industrial waste disposal, agricultural runoff of pesticides and fertilizers, animal waste from factory farms, and faulty sewage treatment facilities. Storm-water runoff from paved areas such as parking lots and streets can contribute to the problem, as can the disposal of household chemicals and medicines down the drain.

Water pollution not only presents a health risk, it also can alter the natural beauty of rivers, lakes, and oceans.

Experiment 4.1

Oil Spills—A Messy Problem

Materials

✓ **an adult**

✓ electronic balance with disposable holders*

✓ permanent marker

✓ scissors

✓ clean feather duster

✓ disposable bowls

✓ measuring cup

✓ water

✓ tablespoon

✓ dishwashing powder

✓ liquid hand soap

✓ dishwashing liquid

✓ laundry powder

✓ new automobile or lawn mower oil (sold where gasoline is sold)

✓ tweezers

✓ paper towels

✓ watch

*This experiment is written assuming that you are allowed to use an electronic balance found in some school science labs. If an electronic balance is not available, then you can try a much simpler procedure given at the end of this experiment. This simple approach may allow you to compare different cleaners, but it will not give you numbers to use to compare their effectiveness. **In either case, you need to have an adult help you with this experiment. When the experiment is complete, be sure to have an adult take the oil to an oil recycling facility. Oil has to be recycled and**

should not be put in the trash or dumped on the ground or down a drain.

Have you ever seen pictures of animals coated with black, sticky oil from an oil spill? The oil can cause many problems for animals. For example, if oil coats a duck's feathers, the duck may not be able to float. Soapy water has been used to remove oil from marine animals and birds. In this experiment, you will try to determine the best type of cleaner for removing oil from feathers.

Make a data table like the one shown in Figure 16. Sample numbers are shown just to help you practice and understand the calculations used to determine items 3, 5, 8, 9, and 10.

Plastic holders (sometimes called weigh boats) are used to weigh objects on an electronic balance. These disposable holders should be available in a school lab that has an electronic balance. Use a permanent marker to label 10 plastic holders A, B, C, D, E, F, G, H, I, and J. Weigh each plastic holder on an electronic balance. Record these masses in the proper location in your data table. A, B, C, D, and E are beside item 1, and F, G, H, I, and J are beside item 6.

Cut 5 feather pieces that are nearly the same off a feather duster—each one should be about the length of your thumb. Place one feather in each of the holders A, B, C, D, and E, and weigh each feather and holder on the electronic balance. Record these masses as item 2 in the data table.

OIL SPILL EXPERIMENT RESULTS

Sample numbers	Mass (g) of measurements with different cleaners				
	Dishwashing powder	Liquid hand soap	Dishwashing liquid	Laundry powder	Water
(1) holder	**A** 1.925	**B**	**C**	**D**	**E**
(2) holder + feather	1.988				
(3) feather = **(2)** − **(1)**	0.063				
(4) holder + feather + oil	2.729				
(5) initial oil = **(4)** − **(2)**	0.741				
(6) holder	**F** 1.905	**G**	**H**	**I**	**J**
(7) holder + feather + oil left	2.203				
(8) feather + oil left = **(7)** − **(6)**	0.298				
(9) oil left = **(8)** − **(3)**	0.235				
(10) % oil removed = $\dfrac{[(5) - (9)] \times 100\%}{(5)}$	68%				

Figure 16.

Data table, calculation equations, and sample numbers for the oil removal experiment are shown in this table.

Use a permanent marker to label five disposable bowls as DISHWASHING POWDER, LIQUID HAND SOAP, DISHWASHING LIQUID, LAUNDRY POWDER, and WATER. Add exactly one cup of water to each bowl. Add one tablespoon of the indicated cleaner to each labeled bowl. The fifth bowl will remain pure water.

Pour a small amount of oil into a sixth disposable bowl. Using tweezers, completely dip the feather from holder A into this bowl of oil. Allow any extra oil to drip off the feather, then touch the feather to a paper towel to get off excess oil. Place the oily feather back in its plastic holder and weigh. Record the total mass beside item 4. Set the feather in a bowl of dishwashing powder. Repeat the same oil dipping and weighing procedures for each of the other feathers. After weighing the feathers, place them in bowls of liquid hand soap, dishwashing liquid, laundry powder, and water.

Allow the five feathers to soak in cleaners for 30 minutes. Use tweezers to swish each feather back and forth 10 times in the cleaner and water control once every 10 minutes. After 30 minutes, remove the feathers from their bowls and place them on separate paper towels. Fold the paper towel over the top of each feather and gently press down for a few seconds to help dry the feather. As indicated in the sample table, you will now need to place each feather as it is weighed into the new holders F, G, H, I, and J. Note that the feathers are moved from holders A to F, B to G, C to H, D to I, and E to J. Find the mass of each holder and feather, and record in item 7.

You should have now recorded masses in your data table beside items 1, 2, 4, 6, and 7. The sample data table gives equations that show you how to do the needed calculations with these numbers. Do these calculations and record the results in items 3, 5, 8, 9, and 10.

The key results are the mass of oil on the feather before cleaning (5) and after (9), and the percent of oil removed (10). The more oil removed, the better the cleaner. If all the oil was removed, item 10 would be 100 percent. If none of the oil was removed, item 10 would be 0 percent. The entire experiment should be repeated several times with new groups of clean feathers, and all the results averaged for each cleaning agent. Compare the percent of oil removed to find the best cleaner for removing oil from feathers. What was the best cleaning agent? Were the agents similar or different in their ability to remove oil?

Huge ships called super tankers move oil across the oceans to many different ports around the world. In 1989, a 300-m- (986-ft-) long oil tanker called the *Exxon Valdez* ran aground and spilled about 11 million gallons of oil into Prince William Sound off the coast of Alaska. Black sticky oil washed onto hundreds of miles of beaches in Alaska. Soapy water was used to clean oil off animals and shorelines after the oil spill. The

Exxon Valdez was one of the most famous oil spills, but there have been many others.

A simpler version of the experiment does not require an electronic balance. Dip three similar feathers in oil. Remove all three feathers. Allow any extra oil to drip off the feathers, then touch each feather to a paper towel to remove excess oil. Place one feather in water, dip another in a tablespoon of dishwasher powder dissolved in a cup of water, and set the third feather aside. Let the feathers soak in water and in the cleaner for 30 minutes, swishing the feathers around a bit every 10 minutes. After 30 minutes, dry with paper towels and compare the three feathers. Can you observe or feel a difference in the feathers? Which feather seems to have the most oil removed? Try other cleaners. Try various amounts of cleaners. Can you find the best cleaner for oily feathers?

Experiment 4.2

Plants and Air Pollutants

Materials

✓ **an adult**

✓ 2 clean dry jars with lids

✓ Strike-Anywhere matches and matchbox

✓ fresh-picked clover plants, stem with leaves (use fresh spinach leaves if you can't find clover)

✓ permanent marker

✓ watch or clock

Are plants sensitive to air pollutants? In this experiment you will study how the air pollutant sulfur dioxide can harm plants.

Ask an adult to help you with this experiment. Do not use matches by yourself.

On a bright, sunny day, collect six clover plants (stems and leaves). Clover is commonly found in lawns and consists of three or four round leaves attached to a stem. Dry the leaves if the plants are damp. You can substitute fresh spinach leaves from a grocery store if you cannot find clover plants.

On one jar write SULFUR DIOXIDE and on the other jar write CONTROL. Remove the lids from both jars. **Ask an adult** to light a match and immediately drop it in the jar labeled sulfur dioxide. Quickly secure the lid on the jar. The match should still be burning while the lid is being tightened.

When the match stops burning and no more smoke is coming from it, open the lid and quickly place three clover plants in the jar. Secure the lid back on the jar.

Place three clover plants in the jar labeled control. Tighten the lid on this jar. Place both jars in a spot that gets plenty of sunshine. Observe the clover plants in each jar every fifteen minutes for one hour. (If you are using spinach, you may want to observe the leaves in the jar for several hours.) Remove the plants from the jars and observe them closely. Describe what happens to the leaves that were in the jar containing sulfur dioxide. Are there any changes in the leaves in the jar labeled control?

Rinse the jar labeled sulfur dioxide several times with water before recycling it or throwing it away.

In this experiment you use matches to generate sulfur dioxide. Sulfur dioxide is one of the six common air pollutants as defined by the U.S. Environmental Protection Agency (EPA). The other five common air pollutants are ozone, nitrogen dioxide, carbon monoxide, lead, and particulate matter. The EPA monitors the levels of these six air pollutants as part of their program to improve the quality of the air we breathe.

Sulfur dioxide is produced during the burning of fossil fuels that contain sulfur. Common fuels that can contain sulfur include oil and coal. Sulfur dioxide is also produced when certain metals are made from their corresponding ores.

Much of the sulfur dioxide that reaches the atmosphere combines with water in the air to form acid rain and acid snow. However, as you discovered in this experiment, sulfur dioxide itself can harm plants. When sulfur dioxide enters the leaves of a plant, it combines with water in the living cells to produce an acid, which in turn damages and can kill the living cells. When the cells in a leaf die, the leaf turns brown. The whole plant can die if sulfur dioxide damages enough leaves.

Science Project Ideas

◊ Are some plant leaves less susceptible to the harmful effects of sulfur dioxide? To find out, repeat this experiment with a variety of plant leaves, including those of evergreens and succulents. For some plant leaves you may need to make your observations over several hours. Make a list of plants and a summary of your observations.

◊ Is sunlight necessary for sulfur dioxide to harm clover plants? How can you find out?

◊ Observe fresh pine needles in various locations around where you live. Pine needles are sensitive to the ground pollutant ozone. Ozone destroys the chlorophyll in pine needles. Pine needles affected by ozone will have yellow blotches covering the needles. Did you find any pine needles with ozone damage?

Experiment 4.3

Plants and Acid Rain

Materials

✓ **an adult**

✓ **6 small identical flowering plants from a nursery
(Cooler vinca plants
work well)**

✓ scissors

✓ permanent marker

✓ 5 plastic cups

✓ index cards

✓ camera

✓ measuring spoon

✓ water

✓ vinegar

Pure rainwater is slightly acidic. However, when it becomes too acidic, it is called acid rain. In this experiment, you will explore what effect the acidity of water can have on growing plants. Do you think more acidic water will help or harm plants?

Obtain six small flowering plants from a nursery or other store that sells plants. The plants should be less than 30 cm (12 in) tall, and as nearly identical as possible. The plants are sold in flat plastic containers with six compartments. **Have an adult** help you cut the plastic flat into six separate containers. Each container will have holes in the bottom to drain excess water.

Use a permanent marker to label five plastic cups A, B, C, D, and E. Select the five plants that seem most identical in size and appearance. Keep the plants in their original containers, but place one plant and its container into each cup.

The containers will fit only partway down each cup (see Figure 17). This arrangement lets excess water drain out of the container into the cup.

Place the five cups in a sunny window, and water the plants following the directions given below. Write the date on an index card and lean the card on the cups. Take one picture of the five plants together, with the card in the photo. In your science notebook, record the date and time and write a brief description of the appearance, shape, and color of the leaves and flowers of each plant.

Water the five cups with the following liquids: A—nothing; B—2 tablespoons of water; C—1½ tablespoons of water and ½ tablespoon of vinegar; D—1 tablespoon of water and 1 tablespoon of vinegar; E—2 tablespoons of vinegar. Each day water the plants in the same way. Plant A gets no water, while each of the other plants gets 2 tablespoons of liquid.

Figure 17.

Plants can be grown inside a soil-filled container inside a plastic cup.

Because vinegar is acetic acid in water, each plant, going from B to C to D to E, receives more acid in its daily watering. Continue the experiment for at least ten days. Each day after you water the plants, take one picture of the five plants together. Be sure to include a new index card with the date in your photo. Write a brief description of the plants each day in your science notebook.

What have you observed after ten days? Did the leaves of some of the plants change color or shape? Have the pictures you took developed and then arrange them in order. What changes do they show? Compare your written descriptions to the pictures. Find out what causes the green color in plant leaves and figure out why the color might change.

Industrial processes—such as burning coal, and car and truck emissions—cause the formation of pollution molecules called sulfur oxides and nitrogen oxides. These molecules combine with water in the air to form nitric and sulfuric acids. In turn, these acids cause rain to be more acidic.

The lower the pH, the more acidic the solution. Neutral water has a pH of 7. Normal rain has a pH of about 5.7 due to dissolved carbon dioxide gas, which forms carbonic acid (see Figure 18). Much of the northeastern part of the United States has rain that is below 4.6 pH, and some places have rain of 4.2 pH. Rain that has a pH of 4.2 has 25 times more acid than normal rain and 630 times more acid than neutral water (pH = 7). Vinegar has a pH of between 2 and 3.

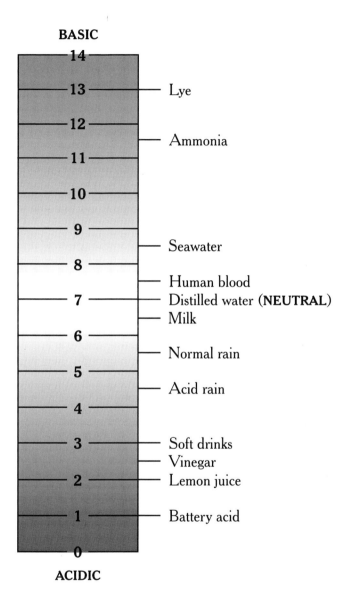

Figure 18.

The pH values of a variety of substances are shown above. A pH value of 5.7 is normal for rain. A pH value of 4.2 to 4.6 is possible for acid rain.

Acid rain is a term that can include acidic rain, snow, fog, and solid particles. It has contributed to the destruction of forests in many places around the world. Acids can wash out essential minerals such as magnesium or help release toxic metals such as mercury from soil or rocks. Excess acid can destroy chlorophyll (green molecules that use sunlight as an energy source for plants). As chlorophyll is destroyed, plants lose their green color and may die. They may be less resistant to damage by insects or bacteria. At low pH, aquatic plants and fish eggs can die. At even lower lake pH, adult fish will die. Many lakes have lost important species of fish, and many trees have been killed because of acid rain.

Maps showing the pH of precipitation around the United States are available on the Internet (http://pubs.usgs.gov/gip/ acidrain/2.html, **or** http://water.usgs.gov/nwc/NWC/pH/ html/ ph.html).

Science Project Idea

Different species of plants grow best in different levels of acidity (see Figure 14 for examples). Try repeating this experiment using water and vinegar mixtures with smaller amounts of vinegar. Can you determine the largest amount of vinegar that has no effect on the plant appearance after two weeks of watering?

Experiment 4.4

Effect of Acid Rain on Materials

Materials

✓ permanent marker	✓ vinegar
✓ 2 small plastic cups	✓ 2 iron nails about 9 cm (3.5 in) long
✓ measuring cup	✓ camera
✓ water	✓ household paint

Can acid rain damage nonliving materials? In this experiment you will use vinegar to simulate acid rain and study its effects on iron.

Use a permanent maker to label one plastic cup VINEGAR and another cup WATER. Add ⅓ cup of water to the cup labeled water and ⅓ cup of vinegar to the cup labeled vinegar. Place an iron nail in each cup (see Figure 19). Only a portion of each nail should be submerged in the liquids. Without disturbing them, observe and record any changes in the nails each day at about the same time for a week. Use a camera to document changes that take place. Be sure to indicate the date in the photo. You may see corrosion (rust) on the nail in the vinegar in just a few hours. Does the corrosion on the nail in the vinegar increase each day? Do you see rust developing on the nail in the water?

Figure 19.

Place one iron nail in a cup containing vinegar and another in a cup containing water. Each day for a week, record any changes you observe in the nails.

Most unprotected metals corrode when exposed to air and water. Acid, like that found in acid rain, can accelerate the corrosion of metals. In this experiment you observed how the acid in vinegar corrodes iron. The amount of acid in vinegar is approximately 100 times more than what is found in acid rain around many urban areas. By using a stronger acid in this experiment, you can observe the corrosive effect of acid on metals more rapidly.

Iron is one of the most abundant metals used to make objects such as bridges, buildings, and automobiles. Most objects made of iron are given a protective coating, such as paint, to prevent corrosion. When iron becomes exposed, it corrodes into rust, which is a crumbly material.

Will household paint protect an iron nail from acid rain? Paint a nail and allow it to dry. Repeat the experiment with the painted nail.

Science Project Ideas

🔥 Repeat this activity using nails or screws made of different metals. Try nails made of aluminum. Try galvanized nails. Try stainless steel screws. Also try pieces of copper wire.

🔥 Stir one teaspoon of vinegar into two cups of water. The water will then be approximately as acidic as the acid rain often recorded around large cities. Repeat the nail experiment with this simulated acid rain. You may find that you will need to make your observations for a longer period of time.

Experiment 4.5

Weather and Air Quality

Materials

✓ the air quality index value each day for two weeks

✓ 14 small sticky notes or pieces paper

Can weather effect air quality? In this activity you will explore the connection between weather and air quality.

You will need to record the air quality index (AQI) value for your community over a span of two weeks. You can find the AQI value in the weather section of most large papers. Some television and radio stations give the day's AQI value as part of their weather broadcast. You can also find AQI values for most of the United States at the Environmental Protection Agency's AIRNow website (http://www.epa.gov/airnow).

The daily AQI value is determined by monitoring five of the major air pollutants: ground-level ozone, carbon monoxide, particulate matter, nitrogen dioxide, and sulfur dioxide. The amount of each air pollutant is measured with specialized instruments that are kept outdoors in the area being monitored. The air pollutant that has the largest AQI value for a particular day determines the AQI value reported for that day. For example, if the AQI value for ozone on a particular day is 46, and the AQI values of the remaining air pollutants are less than 46, then that day's AQI value is reported as 46.

AQI values are reported either as a number from 0 to 500 or as one of six categories. The six categories are good, moderate, unhealthy for sensitive groups, unhealthy, very unhealthy, and hazardous. The relationship between the number values of AQI and the six categories, along with the specific colors assigned to the six categories, is shown in Figure 20.

Air Quality Index (AQI) Values	Air Quality Conditions	Color
0 to 50	Good	Green
51 to 100	Moderate	Yellow
101 to 150	Unhealthy for sensitive groups	Orange
151 to 200	Unhealthy	Red
201 to 300	Very unhealthy	Purple
301 to 500	Hazardous	Maroon

Figure 20.

The table shows the relationship between air quality index (AQI) values and the six categories of air quality.

In your science notebook, divide one page into four equal areas. Label the upper left corner 0–50 GOOD and the upper right corner 51–100 MODERATE. Label the lower left corner 101–150 UNHEALTHY FOR SENSITIVE GROUPS and the lower right corner 151–500 UNHEALTHY TO HAZARDOUS. Each day for fourteen days write on a sticky note the AQI value for the day and, if available, the major pollutant responsible for this AQI value. Also record on the note the general weather conditions for the day. For example, was it sunny and dry, hot and muggy, sunny and windy, cool and damp, or raining? Place the sticky notes in the appropriate AQI area on the notebook paper.

Examine your fourteen-day summary of daily AQI values and weather conditions and note any trends you observe. Generally, weather and the time of year influence air quality. For example, on hot, sunny summer days, the amount of ozone in the atmosphere is usually highest. Ozone (O_3) is a form of oxygen that is produced when exhaust gases and particles from cars, buses, smokestacks, and other sources react with regular oxygen gas (O_2) in the presence of sunlight. In the winter when sunlight is less intense and temperatures are generally lower, less ozone is produced. The pollutant carbon monoxide (CO) results from the incomplete combustion of gasoline and similar fuels. Generally, carbon monoxide levels increase in the cold winter months because combustion of fuels is less complete in cold air. Windy conditions favor increased particle pollution, because the stirring action of the wind can lift and transport particulate matter. Increased sulfur dioxide (SO_2) levels are generally found around industrial plants, such as power plants, that burn sulfur-containing fuels such as coal and oil. Nitrogen dioxide (NO_2) is rarely found as a major air pollutant partly because of better-designed automobile combustion engines.

Science Project Ideas

◊ Repeat this experiment during different times of the year.

◊ Compare the AQI in your area with a nearby city. If you live in a large city, choose a smaller city or town nearby for comparison. If you live in a small city, choose a larger city nearby for comparison. AQI values for cities can be found on the EPA's website.

◊ Compare the AQI values for several different cities around the United States for a period of time. For example, compare the AQI values of Los Angeles, Chicago, and New York City for two weeks. AQI values for these cities can be found at the EPA's website.

Energy Resources— Renewable and Sustainable

Pause for a moment and think about your daily activities. Do any of these activities require the use of energy? The food you eat provides you with energy to live, work, and play. Is energy required to move the food from the farm or the processing plant to the grocery store? Is energy required to cook the food? Did you turn on lights today or use hot water? Do these daily activities require energy? Do the clothes you wear or the books you read require energy to be made?

Amazingly, the average person in the United States consumes approximately 350 million BTU of energy each year!

BTU stands for "British thermal unit" and is a common unit of measure for energy (350 million BTU = 88.2 million Cal = 369.2 million kJ). One BTU is the amount of heat energy required to raise the temperature of one pound of water by one degree Fahrenheit (°F). By way of comparison, 350 million BTU is equivalent to the amount of electrical energy required to burn a single 100-watt lightbulb for 117 years, or to the amount of energy contained in approximately 300,000 average-size candy bars! (That would be an average of 822 candy bars a day.)

Prior to the Industrial Revolution of the late eighteenth century, fire and muscle power from domesticated animals and humans supplied the energy needs of societies. As machines replaced the work done by animals and humans, new sources of energy were needed. Coal provided much of the energy needs during the early years of the Industrial Revolution. Today, coal and the other fossil fuels—oil and natural gas—provide over 80 percent of the world's energy needs. The remainder of the world's energy needs are supplied by nuclear, hydroelectric, geothermal, biomass, solar, wind, and tidal sources.

Fossil fuels are the prehistoric remains of plants and animals that lived over 300 million years ago. The amount of fossil fuels in the earth is limited and cannot be quickly replaced. Fossil fuels are not a renewable source of energy. If we continue to consume fossil fuels at a rapid rate, we will soon deplete this energy source. Thus, there is a growing need to find energy replacements for fossil fuels. These energy replacements need to come from renewable sources, which are formed and regenerated by natural, sustainable processes.

Renewable energy sources used today include solar energy, wind energy, geothermal energy, hydropower, and biomass-derived energy. Solar energy consists of light and heat emitted by the sun. A small fraction of the energy striking the earth each day would provide all of our energy needs, but collecting and storing this energy is challenging. Solar cells, or photovoltaic cells, are used to convert sunlight directly into electricity, which can be used immediately or stored in batteries. Solar thermal collectors capture heat energy from the sun; this can be used to heat water or on a larger scale to generate steam to power an electrical generator.

In effect, wind power is another form of solar energy, since it is the sun's heat that drives the winds. Blades attached to an electrical generator capture the energy associated with moving air. To be effective, wind generators need to be placed in areas that have strong and constant winds.

Several miles below the surface of the earth, there is enough heat to supply the world's energy needs. This heat, called geothermal energy, is released by molten rock called magma. Steam and hot water produced by this heat can be used to generate electricity and to heat buildings.

Hydropower is harnessed by using moving water to turn turbines to generate electricity. The most common and visible hydropower plant consists of a dam and powerhouse containing turbine-driven electrical generators. The movement of water associated with tidal changes is being explored as another type of hydropower.

Biomass is material derived from plants and animals. Heat energy can come from biomass such as wood and peat when it is burned. Biomass can also be converted into liquid fuels such as methanol and ethanol, which can be blended with petroleum-based fuels and burned in transportation vehicles. Methane, which is the chief component of natural gas, is also found in animal wastes and in landfills.

Experiment 5.1

Sun Power

Materials

✓ **an adult**

✓ aluminum pie pan (disposable)

✓ black spray paint (flat, not glossy)

✓ newspaper

✓ measuring cup

✓ water

✓ watch

Have you ever noticed how you can feel the sunshine on your skin on a sunny day? What you feel is the infrared or heat radiation given off by the sun. Sunlight keeps the earth warm, provides light to let us see, powers the water cycle of rain and snow, and provides the energy for green plants to grow. In this experiment, you will measure the heat energy in sunlight and how it varies with time, cloudiness, and season.

Bend part of the edge of a disposable aluminum pie pan to make a spout. The spout will allow you to pour water out of the pie pan without spilling it. Go outside and place the pan on newspaper that is spread on the ground. **Have an adult help you** paint the inside of the pie pan with flat black spray paint. **Do not get the paint on you. Do not breathe the fumes**. Allow the paint to dry overnight.

This experiment needs to be started at about 11:00 A.M. on a warm, sunny day. Place the pie pan in a sunny spot where there is no shade. Use a measuring cup to pour exactly one cup of water into the pie pan. Expose the pan to full sunlight and solar energy for four hours. After exactly four hours, pour the remaining water back into an empty measuring cup to find the volume of water left. How much water remained? Where did the rest of the water go?

Use the solar energy table (see Figure 21) to determine the amount of energy and amount of power observed in your water evaporation experiment. The data in the table allows you to convert the amount of water evaporated during your experiment to the energy used, the power used, and the power per unit area. How many watts per square meter did you observe? Repeat this experiment at least five times, record the individual results, and find the average of your results.

SOLAR ENERGY REQUIRED TO EVAPORATE WATER				
Water Remaining (cup)	Water Evaporated (cup)	Energy Used (joules)	Power Used (watts)	Power per Area (watts/meter^2)
1	0	0	0	0
7/8	1/8	72,250	5	200
3/4	1/4	144,500	10	400
5/8	3/8	216,750	15	600
1/2	1/2	289,000	20	800
3/8	5/8	361,250	25	1,000
1/4	3/4	433,500	30	1,200
1/8	7/8	505,750	35	1,400
0	1	578,000	40	1,600

Figure 21.

This table shows the solar energy used, solar power used, and solar power used per area to evaporate different amounts of water.

Repeat this experiment under different conditions and compare the results. How do the results compare on sunny or cloudy days in the middle of the day in the summer? How do results compare in the late afternoon or early morning in the summer? How do the results compare in the middle of the day in the summer, fall, and spring? How do your results affect the application of solar energy for power generation?

The dark surface of the metal pan absorbs solar energy and becomes warmer. The heat causes water molecules to evaporate and go into the air. As more solar energy strikes the pan, more water evaporates. To understand the energy and the power of sunlight, you will need to understand units of energy and units of power. A dietary calorie (Cal) is equal to 4,184 joules (J) of energy. Therefore a bowl of ice cream that is 240 Cal would have about one million joules of energy [240 Cal × (4184 J/Cal) = 1,004,160 J]. The watt (W) is a unit of power that is defined as one joule per second (J/s). A typical lightbulb uses about 60 or 75W, and an average American home might require thousands of watts of electrical power at times.

It is known that it takes 578,000 J to evaporate one cup of water, and when this number is divided by 14,400 s (the number of seconds in 4 hours), it gives the power in watts. The area of the bottom of a typical pie pan is about 0.025 m² (square meters), and dividing the power (W) by this area (m²) gives the power per square meter of area.

There are many ways that solar energy can be captured and used. Photovoltaic devices can be used to convert sunlight directly to electrical energy, and whole systems can be installed to power homes. Passive solar collectors use water or rocks to store solar heat and can be used to help heat homes and buildings. Solar power also can be used to heat water for washing, bathing, and cleaning. Where there is a shortage of wood or other energy sources for cooking, portable solar collectors with several reflecting surfaces can be used to focus sunlight and cook food.

Experiment 5.2

Electricity From Sunlight

Materials

✓ table

✓ photovoltaic cell with wire leads attached (available at electronics or many science/hobby stores)

✓ multitester that measures voltage and current (available at electronics stores)

✓ a friend

✓ protractor

Can sunlight be converted directly into electricity? In this experiment you will use a photovoltaic cell to generate electricity from sunlight and to explore how the position of the photovoltaic cell relative to the sun influences this conversion. You will measure the amount of current produced by the photovoltaic cell as you vary the angle of elevation of the photovoltaic cell relative to the sun. The angle of elevation is the angle between the horizon and a spot above the horizon. In your science notebook, make a table with two column headings, reading ANGLE IN DEGREES and CURRENT IN MILLIAMPS (see Figure 22). Under angle in

Angle in degrees	Current in milliamps
0	
10	
20	
30	
40	
50	
60	
70	
80	
90	

Figure 22.

Use this table for collecting data from a photovoltaic cell.

degrees, write in the angles you will use in increments of 10, starting with 0 and finishing with 90.

Do this activity outside on a flat, level table on a bright sunny day. Attach an insulated wire to each lead coming from a photovoltaic cell. Attach one of these wires to the red test wire and the other wire to the black test wire coming from the multi-tester (it does not matter which wire from the photovoltaic cell is attached to the red test wire on the multitester). Set the multitester to read the current in milliamps. Turn the multitester on.

Ask a friend to hold a protractor straight up with the bottom edge flat on the table. Make sure the horizontal axis of the protractor is pointed in the direction of the sun (see Figure 23). **Never look directly at the sun!** Next, place the photovoltaic cell flat on the table (make sure the proper side of the cell is pointed up). Measure the current generated, and record this value in your table next to the angle of 0 degrees. While holding the photovoltaic cell next to the protractor, lift the end of the cell

Figure 23.

Measure the amount of current generated by the photovoltaic cell at different angles of elevation relative to the sun.

farthest from the sun up to an angle of 10 degrees. Measure the current generated and record it in your table. Repeat this process for each angle in your table. Make a plot of your data with *angle in degrees* on the x-axis and *current in milliamps* on the y-axis (see Figure 24). Based on your graph, is there an optimal angle of elevation or range of optimal angles of elevation of the photo-voltaic cell that generates the most current?

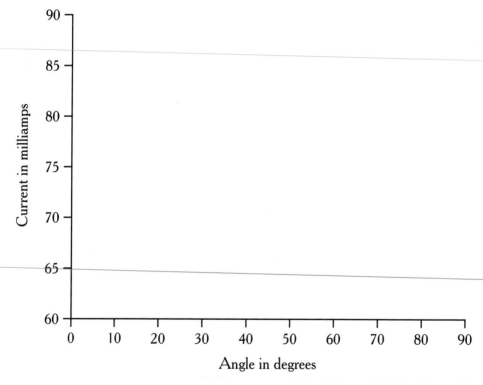

Figure 24.

Plot the current in milliamps versus angle of elevation.

Photovoltaic cells, also called solar cells, were first developed to provide power for satellites and spacecraft. Today they are used in many applications, including solar-powered calculators, radios, highway emergency telephones, and outdoor lights.

The most common photovoltaic cells consist of two chemically different thin layers of silicon, which are sandwiched together. One of these layers of silicon contains added boron and is called the positive layer, or P-layer. The other silicon layer contains added phosphorous and is called the negative layer, or N-layer. The addition of boron and phosphorous to silicon is called doping.

When sunlight strikes a photovoltaic cell, some of the energy in the light is absorbed by the silicon atoms, which knocks electrons loose from these atoms. These electrons can move freely, and if the wires attached to the photovoltaic cell are attached to a circuit, electrons will flow, creating a current.

For optimal performance, solar panels must be positioned toward the sun and should be inclined at an angle that allows the solar panels to absorb the maximum amount of sunlight. This angle of inclination changes from morning to evening and from season to season, so adjustments in this angle have to be made. Some solar panels are mounted on tracking systems that keep them optimally pointed toward the sun. The International Space Station uses drive motors to turn its solar panels, so they are always facing the sun. These solar panels, consisting of nearly 300,000 photovoltaic cells, supply all the station's electrical needs.

Science Project Ideas

- Repeat this activity at different times of the day. Does the angle of inclination for maximum current production change from morning to noon or from morning to late afternoon?

- Using your measurements at the optimal angle of inclination, compare the amount of current generated on a sunny day with the amount of current generated on a cloudy day.

- Repeat this activity at different times of the year.

- Can a photovoltaic cell generate electricity from moonlight? To find out, try this activity on a clear night when the moon is full.

Experiment 5.3

Electricity From Wind

Materials

✓ **an adult**

✓ battery-operated portable fan

✓ multitester that measures voltage and current (available at electronics store)

✓ 2 wires with alligator clips attached to each end

✓ a friend

✓ ruler

✓ multispeed electric room fan

✓ table

Can the force in wind be used to generate electricity? In this activity you will use a battery-operated fan to explore how the energy of moving air can be converted into electricity.

You will need a battery-operated personal fan for this activity. The Squeeze Breeze® brand of personal fan works well because it has large foam blades for capturing moving air. The Squeeze Breeze® personal fan can be found at many large retail stores or can be ordered over the Internet.

Remove the propeller from the shaft of the battery-operated fan. **Ask an adult to help you remove the small motor from the housing of the fan.** Carefully reattach the propeller to the shaft of the motor. Attach wires to each of the two leads on the housing of the motor. Attach one of these wires to the red test wire and the other to the black test wire coming from a multitester. It does not matter which wire is attached to the red test wire on the multitester.

Ask a friend to help you with this activity. Make a table like the one in Figure 25 for collecting your data.

Place a room fan on a table and set the fan speed to medium. Place a ruler in front of the fan. Turn the multitester on and set it to read DC (direct current) volts. Hold the motor and propeller assembly (wind generator) in front of the fan (see Figure 26). Move the wind generator backward, forward, and side to side until you find a maximum reading of volts on the multitester. Continue to hold the wind generator in the place where you get the maximum reading. Ask your friend to write down how far the wind generator is from the fan, and to record the volts observed with the fan speed on medium. Ask your friend to switch the multitester to read current in milliamps and

Fan Speed	Volts Generated	Milliamps Generated	Microwatts Generated
Low	0.44	0.2	88
Medium	0.54	1	540
High	0.60	2	1200
Distance between fan and wind generator is 6 inches.			

Figure 25.

Organize data from the wind generator in a table.

Figure 26.
Hold the wind generator in front of the fan.

to record the current while you hold the wind generator in place. Repeat these measurements with the fan speed set on low and on high. To calculate how much power in microwatts your wind generator produces, multiply the volts by the milliamps for the given fan speed setting.

The data in the table shown in Figure 25 were obtained using a room fan with a 12-inch-diameter fan blade. Your results may vary depending on the size of your fan and the size of the motor in your battery-operated portable fan. A plot of the data in this table is shown in Figure 27.

Energy is the ability to do work. If you have ever seen a sailboat skim across the surface of a lake, being pushed only by the wind, you know that moving air or wind contains energy. In fact, humans have used wind energy to do work for centuries. In addition to harnessing the wind to move large sail-driven ships around the world, humans have used windmills to pump

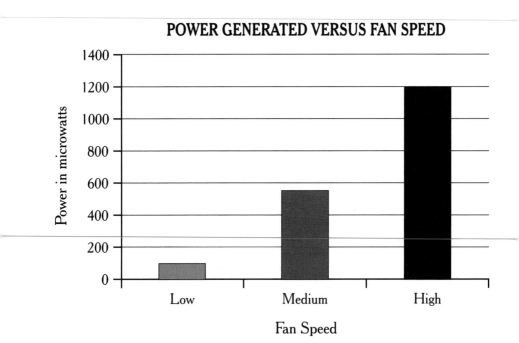

Figure 27.
Plot the microwatts of power versus fan speed.

water from the ground and to drive simple gristmills to grind grain. Today, wind generators around the world are used to harness the energy in wind to make electricity. Wind is becoming increasingly popular as a source of electricity because using wind to generate electricity is both clean and renewable.

Wind is created by the uneven heating of the earth's surface by the sun. Thus, wind energy is actually a form of solar energy. To be economical, wind generators need to be in locations where wind speeds average between 12 and 18 mph. Although only 6 percent of the United States has suitable wind speeds, it is estimated that with properly designed wind farms in these areas, enough electricity could be generated to supply all the current electricity needs of the United States.

The blades of a wind generator are what capture the kinetic energy contained in winds. Kinetic energy is the energy of motion. The blades turn a driveshaft, creating mechanical energy that turns an electrical generator. The generator converts the mechanical energy into electrical energy. As you learned in this experiment, the faster the wind, the more power that can be generated.

Science Project Ideas

⧫ Repeat this activity with fans of different sizes.

⧫ Use a handheld wind speed indicator (available at an electronics stores) to determine the wind speeds generated by your fan at the low, medium, and high settings. Make sure to measure the wind speeds at the same position in front of the fan where you made your measurements with the multitester. Make a plot of milliamps versus wind speed. The wind speeds of the fan used to develop this activity were 11, 13, and 15 miles per hour at the settings of low, medium, and high, respectively.

⧫ Try your wind generator outside on a windy day. How much power in milliamps does it generate?

Experiment 5.4

Heat From Decaying Grass Clippings

Materials

✓ **an adult**

✓ fresh grass clippings

✓ 2 empty 1-L plastic drink bottles with caps

✓ 19-L (5-gal) bucket

✓ water

✓ instant-read thermometer

✓ clock or watch

Biomass is the organic material made by living things. When a dead plant or animal decomposes, complex chemical substances are broken down into simpler chemical substances. These chemicals nourish the soil, so the life cycle can continue. As part of this chemical breakdown, heat energy is generated. Can decaying grass clippings release enough energy to heat a quantity of water?

Ask an adult to collect fresh grass clippings after mowing the grass. Using a 19-L (5-gal) bucket as a measure, make a pile of approximately 114 L (30 gal) of grass clippings in a shaded area in the yard. Fill a 1-L plastic drink bottle with water. Place the cap on the bottle, but do not secure tightly—leave the cap loose. Make a well in the top of the grass pile large enough for the water bottle. Place the water bottle in the well and lightly pack grass clippings around the bottle until only the cap is showing (see Figure 28). Fill a second 1-L drink bottle with water and lightly cap it. Set this bottle of water in the shade next to the pile of grass. This bottle will serve as a control.

Remove the cap from each bottle and measure and record the temperature (°F) of the water in each bottle. Make sure to record the time and date of your measurements. Replace the caps, making sure to leave them loose. If possible, measure

experiment bottle

grass clippings

control bottle

Figure 28.

Place a 1-L plastic bottle nearly full of water in a pile of grass clippings. For a control, place another nearly full 1-L plastic bottle next to the pile of grass clippings. Both should be in the shade.

and record the temperature in each bottle in the morning, at midday, and in the evening for several days. Always record the time and date of your measurements. **The water in the plastic bottle in the pile of grass clippings can get very hot, so avoid burning yourself.** Make a plot of your data with hours on the x-axis and temperature on the y-axis (see Figure 29). How hot did the water get in the bottle stored in the grass clippings? How long did it take for this water to reach its maximum temperature? How many days does this water remain hot? By how much does the temperature of the water in the control bottle vary?

A typical home water heater is set to give water at the faucet between 120°F (49°C) and 160°F (71°C). How hot did your water get?

Biomass is a renewable energy source, since it comes from living things. This experiment shows that energy is released when biomass decomposes. Energy from biomass can be obtained in other ways as well. For example, wood and certain agricultural residues can be burned to produce heat. This heat can then be used to generate electricity. Also, certain forms of biomass can be converted into ethanol, which can be used as a fuel to power vehicles.

Most of the energy needs of the world are derived from fossil fuels such as oil, natural gas, and coal. There is a growing worldwide concern that the burning of fossil fuels is contributing to environmental problems such as acid rain and global

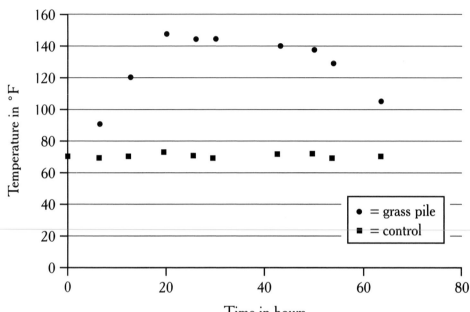

Figure 29.

Make a plot of temperature versus time for the water in each 1-L bottle.

warming. Many people believe that deriving more of our energy from biomass can help alleviate these environmental problems.

Science Project Ideas

- Repeat this experiment using half the amount of grass clippings (57 L, or 15 gal). How does the plot of this data compare with your plot using 114 L (30 gal) of grass clippings?

- How much water can you heat with 114 L (30 gal) of grass clippings? Place a 3.8-L (1-gal) plastic container of water in the grass clippings and see how hot the water gets. Repeat this experiment with containers holding 7.6 L (2 gal), 11.4 L (3 gal), and 15.2 L (4 gal) of water.

- Is heat generated in the decomposition of leaves?

SCIENCE SUPPLY COMPANIES

Carolina Biological Supply Company
2700 York Road
Burlington, NC 27215-3398
(800) 334-5551
http://www.carolina.com

Connecticut Valley Biological
Supply Company
82 Valley Road
P.O. Box 326
Southampton, MA 01073
(800) 628-7748
http://www.ctvalleybio.com

Delta Education
80 Northwest Boulevard
P.O. Box 3000
Nashua, NH 03061-3000
(800) 442-5444
http://www.delta-education.com

Edmund Scientifics
60 Pearce Avenue
Tonawanda, NY 14150-6711
(800) 728-6999
http://scientificsonline.com

Educational Innovations, Inc.
362 Main Avenue
Norwalk, CT 06851
(888) 912-7474
http://www.teachersource.com

Fisher Science Education
4500 Turnberry Drive
Hanover Park, IL 60133
(800) 955-1177
http://www.fisheredu.com

Frey Scientific
100 Paragon Parkway
Mansfield, OH 44903
(800) 225-3739
http://www.freyscientific.com/

NASCO-Fort Atkinson
901 Janesville Avenue
P.O. Box 901
Fort Atkinson, WI 53538-0901
(800) 558-9595
http://www.nascofa.com/

NASCO-Modesto
4825 Stoddard Road
P.O. Box 3837
Modesto, CA 95352-3837
(800) 558-9595
http://www.nascofa.com

Sargent-Welch/VWR Scientific
P.O. Box 5229
Buffalo Grove, IL 60089-5229
(800) 727-4386
http://www.sargentwelch.com

Science Kit & Boreal Laboratories
777 East Park Drive
P.O. Box 5003
Tonawanda, NY 14150
(800) 828-7777
http://sciencekit.com

Ward's Natural Science
P.O. Box 92912
Rochester, NY 14692-9012
(800) 962-2660
http://www.wardsci.com

Further Reading

Dobson, Clive, and Gregor Gilpin Beck. *Watersheds: A Practical Handbook for Healthy Water.* Tonawanda, N.Y.: Firefly Books, Limited, 1999.

Krautwurst, Terry, Gwen Diehn, Joe Rhatigan, Heather Smith, and Alan Anderson. *Nature Smart: Awesome Projects to Make With Mother Nature's Help.* New York: Main Street Publishers, 2004.

Morgan, Sally. *Alternative Energy Sources.* Chicago, Ill.: Heinemann Library, 2002.

Parks, Peggy J. *Global Warming.* San Diego, Calif.: Lucent Books, 2003.

Taylor, Barbara. *How to Save the Planet.* New York: Scholastic Library Publishing, 2001.

Walker, Pam, and Elaine Wood. *Ecosystem Science Fair Projects Using Worms, Leaves, Crickets, and Other Stuff.* Berkeley Heights, N.J.: Enslow Publishers, Inc., 2005.

Internet Addresses

The Globe Program. *Student Investigations.*
<http://www.globe.gov/fsl/investigations/ArchiveReports.pl?
archtype=normallang=en&nav=1>

U.S. Environmental Protection Agency.
<http://www.epa.gov>

U.S. Environmental Protection Agency. *Science Fair Fun.*
<http://www.epa.gov/epaoswer/osw/kids/pdfs/
sciencefair.pdf>

Index